# Hands that Created Our Heritage

*History only exists if the stories are told and recorded.*

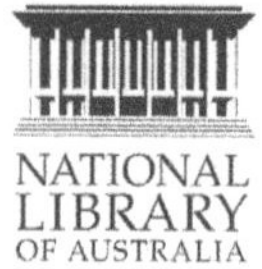


A catalogue record for this book is available from the National Library of Australia



For information about this title or to order other books and/or electronic media, contact the publisher:

Permission was granted to the author at the time of interview, to use images, stories and quotes for public display and publication by the subjects in this book – 2015-2019.

All images were taken in various locations within Australia

**Publisher:**
ASPG (Australian Self Publishing Group)
P.O. Box 159, Calwell, ACT Australia 2905
Email: publishaspg@gmail.com
http://www.inspiringpublishers.com

National Library of Australia Cataloguing-in-Publication entry

Author: Harpell, Lexa

Title: **HANDS THAT CREATED OUR HERITAGE**/*Lexa Harpell.*

Cover design by Lexa Harpell

Photographic images by Lexa Harpell and Roberta

ISBN: 978-1-922327-23-9 (print)

# Contents

# Acknowledgement

*I'd like to begin by respectfully acknowledging the traditional custodians of this land of Indigenous people both past and present, on which we live in today.*

*Respecting their culture and the often important role Indigenous people played during these mentioned early years in our incredible country. Their rich cultural heritage is yet another story to be told and recorded.*

# Dedication

*A huge, heartfelt thank you to all the people who shared their treasured, intimate life stories with me.*

*For your generous warmth and openness to a 'blow in' city girl.*

*Hearing your stories changed my perspective on life and gave me a greater appreciation for our amazing country and its past.*

*Your hard work created a comfortable life for future generations.*

*Your hand's work and pioneering efforts has not gone unnoticed.*

*Your stories will be remembered through time.*

# Change is constant

Around 180 million years ago, the supercontinent of Gondwana split into various landforms and drifted across the globe. One landform wandered further than all and found its way deep in the southern oceans and became known as the continent of Australia. Because of this remote geographical separation, distinctive fauna and flora began evolving, unlike anywhere else on the planet. Australia was slowly creating its own uniqueness.

For the past tens of thousands of years, the established population of Indigenous people lived a life in harmony that was at one with all nature.

In 1788, this land was about to dramatically change both visually and culturally when European colonisation began with the First Fleet of 1,500 convicts. They were brought to this country to be used as free labour to establish the foundation of modern Australia. To carve this land in a way Europeans were accustomed. By 1868 around 162,000 convicts had been transported to Australia along with over one million free settlers from various countries around the world.

Australia is unique as our Indigenous people are the oldest living culture on our planet and European colonisation is one of the youngest. Two vastly opposing humanities desperately trying to find a way to live together harmoniously on this ancient land.

Early settlers were unaware that Australia was the most arid occupied continent on the earth with extreme, unpredictable weather patterns. Due to its age, this remote vast land held some of the most nutrient deficient soils for agriculture. A massive challenge and an immense contrast to what they knew in their homelands. However, they courageously persisted to carve a life and ultimately, a nation with an unforgiving land that was before them.

***We owe much to our early hardy and spirited people.***

***Against many harsh odds, they laid the foundation of modern Australia by hand for which we greatly benefit today.***

# My Journey of Discovery

After spending several months in Europe visiting the towns of our family's ancestors, I had a great urge to travel in my own country with a purpose of some kind. Through the eyes of a 'tourist', rather than a complacent familiarity. To witness and understand the country itself and who we are as Australians.

A long forgotten idea sparked which took me around Australia to hear stories from a fascinating collection of people. A time when our hands connected us to life and were the most important tools we possessed. I wasn't quite sure what would emerge from these conversations, I only knew I wanted to hear the stories of their lives and I had absolutely no clue how, where it would lead or what it would illustrate.

When you have a strong desire to do something, a series of unexpected events enter your world to set you on your journey. Within my last week in a small rural town in Ireland, I heard a story of a man who travelled Ireland's west coast in a campervan photographing the magnificent coastline. The word 'campervan' burnt in my mind.

I had no idea what a campervan looked like, so I quickly scanned the internet to find an ideal mode of transport for my journey. Filled with blind faith and oblivious of what life would be like living 'on the road'. Where to begin my search, how to locate the people I wanted to speak with swirled through my mind. Then I remembered an Irish ballad of a father sent to Tasmania for seven years as a convict for stealing a few ears of corn to feed his family. There was no time to second guess or think, just a lot of action to make this happen and a good dose of trust.

Within weeks of arriving back in Australia, I was heading to our island state of Tasmania whilst frantically learning about this new transient lifestyle. This was a major stretch for me, as I was a city girl through and through. Armed with the barest of essentials and my much needed technology; my laptop and camera gear. It was a very steep learning curve, especially about how to acquire power and water and locate campsites each day.

Along the way, I also wanted to photo journal the breathtaking diverse landscapes to record the uniqueness of our country.

***I had an amusing thought...***
***a modern day 'Waltzing Matilda' roaming the country.***

***Instead of walking, I was driving***
***and my swag - my 'Matilda' was my second hand, compact campervan.***

# Who was I looking for?

My focus was to speak with people born around 1920 to 1935 who belonged in the Greatest and Silent Generations. People who manually worked the land, were touching the land or life in some form on a daily basis.

Trying to find a specific group of people to interview in this enormous country was like finding needles in a very large haystack. You just had to systematically rummage through the pile piece by piece, asking thousands of people until you find them. I eventually learnt the smaller the town the better chances I had to uncover the people I was seeking. People who were willing to spend time with me and share their intimate life stories.

Generally speaking, these generations were the last group of people who carved the foundation of modern Australia with their bare hands, using the simplest of manual tools before hi-tech machinery. They were also highly influential in creating our identity, our heritage.

They witnessed and lived through more changes in their single life than perhaps any other throughout history. From horseback to man on the moon. From hand written letters to the world of instant communication, the internet. They adjusted and accepted the many changes in their lives in silence. Not complaining, just 'getting on with it', regardless of the hardships, challenges or setbacks.

Many had little to no formal education, yet they were well educated in the school of life. They developed a variety of skills and gained valuable knowledge to survive and work. They learnt about the seasons, weather, the land and all living forms. They were in touch with the land and life itself on a daily basis.

***They were connected to life through their hands***
***and this land became a part of themselves.***

They grew up quickly and took on adult responsibilities when they were just children. It was all hands on learning and most knew they could adapt to each new task which was given to them.

Learning that many Aboriginal people played a large role in this part of our history than we had been taught in school. In the Outback, they were spoken of in such high regard by many and pivotal to the great success of the cattle industry.

This group of people were born around The Depression era in the 1920's, experiencing the harsh effects of a paltry existence. Eager to change the life of their parents, they saw opportunities in this vast, raw land. To put food on the table and build a life, they needed to be flexible and front up for any style of work, no matter how menial. At times they had little choice, often moving where there was work. Some travelled seasonally, others from state to state, a good number travelled from across the globe. Other roles were born out of necessity or their surrounds. Most communally, they began their working life as mere children.

The attitude was, if you didn't work, you didn't eat. It was that simple. There were few if any handouts and most would not accept anything as long as they were physically able to work. They were proud people, adopting strong values and strong work ethics.

Just as life began to look promising, a devastating World War broke out when many were at the age to participate in some way. Eagerly raising their hands to take action, they saw it as their duty to their country, the Commonwealth, their families and their values. They had little hesitation to defend their beliefs. Their life and dreams went on hold for several years. The war ended and those who survived and retuned home, picked up the pieces of their life to start over again. Within a few years, the new era of technology emerged which grew at a rapid rate. People had to adjust to another way of life, yet again.

Their life was constantly changing and adapting to life's dramatic events. Yet they did so in silence and with an acceptance.

***This is why this generation became known as***
***'The Silent Generation'.***

# What did I find?

Each time I met with people for my quest, I would explain my purpose and then wait to hear their story unfold. A story that was significant to them about their life. With the anticipation of not knowing what each story would reveal, every moment was filled with the excitement of unwrapping an unexpected gift.

Intently observing their well-worn, etched faces relax as they began to comb through their memories. A proud, tender smile gently swept across their face. As each story enfolded, I found they spoke in a matter of fact manner, devoid of ego or self-image. The stories didn't appear to be glamourised or embellished, just retelling them in a casual, factual style. Many moments were filled with humorous laughter as they spoke of their obstacles, hardships and even the dangers.

Recounting their early life, most softly uttered; *'it was a hard life'*, strongly emphasising the word *'hard'*. A life that was physically tough on their bodies and hands in the harshest of conditions. Yet each person affectionately grinned when they said they would not change their life and would do it all again. Each appeared to possess a subtle sense of pride, satisfied with their life's endeavours. That complete acceptance of life in silence kept strongly emerging.

Being well aware we tend to romanticise the memories of our youth with *'Ah they were the good old days'* or comparing a life to the current times with a *'back in our day it was different'*. Interestingly, those kind of referenced words weren't voiced and in their stories. Lacking the romantic delusions, self-interest or bragging, they were retold with an honest, modest account of their life, just how it happened, nothing more.

Their world appeared to express simple, strong values. A solid sense of pride, mateship, community and honour emanated from each person. Their word was their truth.

Life was modest, although tough. They had more time for their families and friends yet they worked more. The pace was strangely slower, yet more effective as it was not complicated or filled with unnecessary activities. It was focused with few deviations. Interestingly, they didn't talk about stress in their life, they just saw it as hardships.

They didn't care to see a doctor unless they had a major injury they couldn't mend themselves. Using simple home remedies rather than medication, torn rags were their bandages. Sometimes, I jokingly asked if they needed sleeping pills! Their reaction to this seemingly absurd question was always a hearty laugh. Responding that they were so exhausted at the end of each day, they ate dinner and slept deeply until the sun came up.

Food for them was merely sustenance. With little choice, they ate whatever was available to fill their stomachs and fuel their bodies. Overindulgence wasn't part of their life as their bodies were usually fit and lean. It was a simplistic, predictable diet. The large amounts of fats and starches they consumed were burnt off with their constant physical activity.

In essence, they just didn't sweat the small stuff, they did what was needed and got on with their tasks and life. They daren't whinge if they were too tired, too sick, or something was too hard, it would fall on deaf ears of those around them. 'Just get on with it' would be the answer. It appeared to be an uncomplicated, productive life.

Listening to each story unfold, I strained to visualise myself in their shoes. It was very difficult to fathom at times. The differences in our life styles seemed like an enormous leap in time, occurring in just one or two short generations. I wondered how did we become so 'soft' and out of touch so rapidly. These how's and why's posed many questions which intensified my curiosity about this generation.

## *Observing hands is intriguing*

***Hands reveal clues about the person and their work.***
***They are individual road maps created from a life well lived***
***that hold a rich and colourful history.***

Their work was done with a willing and eager set of hands. Active and busy all day long, they touched and experienced all forms of 'life'. Over time they may have slowed, become less nimble, weathered, scarred and some parts broken. Yet these highly complex and relatively fragile part of our body never wore out from a lifetime of hard work.

Everyday people's stories are invaluable in understanding our history and in some ways ourselves. They give more of an intimate insight into life and the hardships many endured for our benefit today.

Quite a number of these people had not told their life stories to anyone for decades, some never at all.

Soon, this group of people won't be around to share their insights about our history and that deeper understanding of our heritage. The era of the creation of our foundation is slipping away. Countless hands from many prior generations carved the foundation of modern Australia and created our heritage. Their life and work is their legacy to us and future generations.

***These stories are part of our heritage; and history only exists***
***if the stories are told and recorded.***

# What did I learn?

Growing up in a multicultural suburb of Sydney from the 1960's, I was exposed to a stimulating array of accents and foods which created a curiousness about people and the world. An Italian family also began living next door to our home when I was about 10 years old. We often exchanged plates of food to each other over the back fence and joined in each family's celebrations. I saw life as a wonderful cultural exchange of learning.

My parents weren't particularly religious, yet urged me to visit the varied places of worship in our area. In their way, they were telling me to learn and understand differences and to explore views and thoughts. It felt as if I was constantly tasting what the world offered and thought everyone had the same experience. This smorgasbord of nationalities and diverse ways of life was exciting for me as a child. My mind was actively absorbing a broad range of information propelling my constant curiosity. From a young age, I understood through my experience that Australia was made up of many nationalities.

Looking back, our school curriculum on Australia's history was limited to say the least and I hadn't really understood how we developed our identity. Subtle thoughts of our unique traits continued to build throughout my life which always sat at the back of my mind.

So this journey was a natural extension to add more pieces of the broader puzzle together and to understand the variety of features of why and who we are as Australians.

I've always relished change, believing change is parallel to growth and learning. My travels around Australia enriched my life further in oh so many ways. It created a different perspective on life, how we live today and how I will live in the future. What I will change and try in some way to combine the best of each generation.

The no fuss, simpler life became easy to me. Gaining a deep appreciation for our history, our culture and the people who created this foundation. I gained a profound love of our incredibly striking, diverse country. I managed to witness and experience some of the great natural wonders on this planet in our 'home', Australia whilst capturing incredible sights through my photography.

This journey also created a strong desire to learn and understand more about our rich Indigenous culture and history from meeting and speaking with many Aboriginal people along the way.

Engaging with the multitude of international travellers who travel our country allowed me to keep looking at Australia 'through the eyes of a tourist' in innocent wonder.

Exposing the seedier side our history was harsh. Yet we can't afford to sugar coat life or pretend it didn't happen, otherwise we can't learn from our mistakes, move forward and grow.

It was an absolute pleasure to have met and hear these personal stories from remarkable people. I will always cherish my time spent with them, although there were some sad moments.

While travelling in New South Wales, I'd heard about a gentleman who was a Rat of Tobruk in WWII. He lived in a small country town about 400kms away. Eager to hear his stories, I quickly changed direction to find and speak with him. Sadly, he'd passed away just two weeks before I arrived. I just hope he shared his valuable stories with someone.

As I continued my travels, I heard that one gentleman I had met in the Outback had passed away a few days after we met. It was devastating news to hear a few months later and didn't expect my emotional attachment. I blubbered and cried for days. Isolating myself for a week just to be in my thoughts. This man only begun to tell his stories to family members within his last year. I felt deeply honoured and blessed he shared some of them with me and ultimately you.

Too many times I'd heard *"You should have been here a few years ago, but the oldies from around here are all gone now."* or *"Oh old so and so pioneered this area, he had some stories, he passed on a little while ago."* The reality of time passing set in and created a sense of urgency to continue my search.

As sad as it was to hear these comments, I was immensely grateful for the people I did manage to meet to hear and record their stories.

I hope this will create an interest with some readers to take time to listen to the stories of our elderly population and record the stories in their own family, community or country. People are our living history and they have much to impart on life. If we just stop and take the time.

Enjoy reading these stories and in your own way, gain some insight and an appreciation for our early generations. What it took to build the foundation of this country or create a desire to explore our incredible country's landscapes.

That niggling question lingered in the back of my mind. What forged our unique traits, identity and what is our heritage?

***This journey allowed me put those pieces together and prompted me to understand exactly what is our heritage and how was it shaped.***

# What is our Heritage and how was it shaped?

I'd never really thought a great deal about our heritage or what it took to build a productive nation. After listening to the stories of its people, uncovering parts of our history and a lot of research, I learnt with an inquisitiveness.

Our heritage is rich and varied. It covers many features rolled into a word or thought, which create our own uniqueness. It is portrayed through our stories, our spirit and ingenuity, values and traditions. Our diverse cultures, historic events, buildings and our distinctive timeless landscape.

Our indigenous people continually gives us a solid ancient connection to the land. British colonisation gives us a structure with a democratic, western law. And our varied range of migrants enrich our country's diversity.

The foundation of modern Australia is pioneering, rewarding and often brutally unforgiving. Our heritage expresses our identity, giving us an understanding to learn where we have come from and who we are as a nation.

Our indigenous people were treated harshly. Our convicts did not want to be here, they had no choice. Early settlers chose to create a new life in a very unfamiliar land, either out of necessity or sense of adventure, leaving behind all they knew half way across the world. The vast majority would never return home or ever see their families again.

This new life would be a 'make or break' existence. They would have to draw deeply on all their own characteristics and continually adapt to the ever changing situations. Many dug deep into their spirit and rose above their challenging events. Sadly, some succumbed to the often brutal conditions and situations, paying the ultimate price with their life.

They created traits of an early identity of mateship, fair play, resourcefulness, courage and independence. Stemming from their physical and mental isolation within Australia and to the rest of the world, including a great need to survive in a strange, new land.

A strong belief in classlessness, scepticism and a dislike of authority was developed. This derived from our ugly convict period, which rolled into our deep admiration for our notorious Bushrangers. In ways these traits still exists today.

***'Perhaps seeing the worst in humanity caused a rebellion that encouraged Australians to seek the best in it; Australia's weaknesses thus became its strengths.'***

*From: Chronicle of Australia 2000*

Australians developed a wicked ability to laugh at themselves and being a bit of a larrikin, most likely to offset their many adversities. They prized physical competence, hard work and the outdoors.

There was a sense of physical and mental freedom as they were now far from traditional restrictions or historical reference of their ancestral homes. They saw opportunities and basically were able to be their own person, to do things their own way with a strong innate sense of themselves. They became layback, modest and with a steely individualism. They worked towards a quality of life rather than status.

With sheer persistence, they explored and pioneered new areas across this remote, immense country. They laid the foundation with backbreaking work using their bare hands to feed us by creating various types of farms and livestock stations. Uncovering the land's mineral wealth, they dug mines manually. Clearing land to link our communication with roads, railway tracks and telegraph lines using a pick and shovel, while living rough in the environment. Building homes, towns, cities and ultimately a productive nation in a relatively short period of time.

In less than 100 years, Australia became an abundant food bowl for the rest of the world. They also became highly creative inventors developing a unique style of ingenuity. They had left behind traditional ways opening new thoughts and ideas. Our heritage was strongly evolving.

They bravely defended our country, the Commonwealth and our way of life across the globe in many wars with their precious lives. They became known as spirited and modest, fighting in a fearless style, like no other.

Failure itself was not feared or looked down upon. Winning against others was also not the highest priority. The endeavour of not giving up or giving it a go against the odds was the prize. 'Give it a go' became synonymous with Australians. We are still known today to take on the hard challenges in life regardless of the outcome. That unique spirit lives on. Our current generation have adapted the phrase in line with our modern language with 'Give it a crack'.

Our informality allowed people to be taken just as they are and to have a reasonable opportunity to do or have something. Giving everyone a 'fair go' resonated throughout the land.

Our identity may have altered slightly over recent years, yet this collection of traits are our core, moulded by early Australian people. You can see these entrenched traits today displayed in many fields of endeavour with our athletes, scientists, military, inventors, farmers, the arts, business as well as people in everyday of life.

Without the great efforts of our many early people, Australia would not be in this envied position today and our life would be very different.

***Their bold spirit and colourful stories capture***
***a part of our Australian identity.***
***Their stories need to be heard and recorded.***

# HANDS THAT CREATED OUR HERITAGE

*History only exists if the stories are told and recorded*

These hands have a tale to tell.

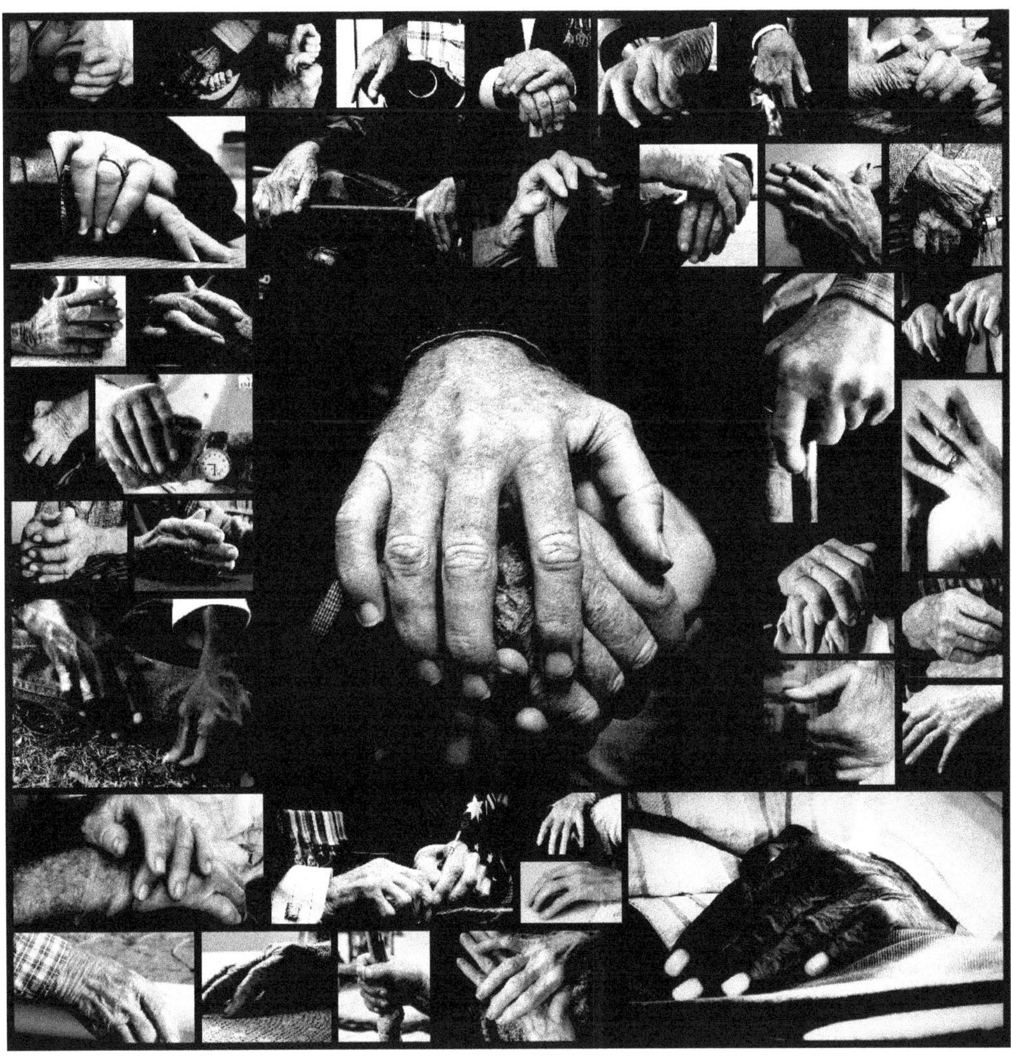

# Discovering Secrets in Tasmania

The first thing you notice about Tasmania is nature's beautiful soft colour palate. Pastel blue sky and waters, white sands and mustard green tones. It felt like entering another country. You also notice the containment of the state. You only had to drive an hour and you are already somewhere and those 'somewheres' were a diverse range of exciting, colourful landscapes. Tasmania is a pristine hiking paradise attracting people from all over the world to explore its stunning natural beauty of mountains, coastlines and wooded forests.

Our island state of Tasmania was originally named Van Diemen's Land where over forty percent of Australia's convicts were sent in the early 1800's. The 65,000 convicts comprised of men, women and children, mainly from Britain and Ireland.

In a dark bizarre way, it was a clever idea by the British authorities to use convicts to quickly build a colony, however it was an utterly inhuman exploitation of human life. Put to work as virtual slaves, free labour to build that foundation of modern Australia in some of the most appalling conditions. Not all convicts were drunken, troublesome, murders or professional thieves. A good number stole out of necessity - minor amounts of food to feed themselves or their starving families, or stole garments just to keep warm. The minimum sentence for these small offences was seven years transportation.

Tasmania is an intriguing place to explore and to learn more about our rich convict past. It is home to numerous, beautifully preserved World Heritage Listed Convict Sites which dot across the state. Tasmania built a total of seven penal colonies, more than any other state.

Numerous male convicts were assigned to work in chain gangs for public works such as the Hobart Wharf, others were less fortunate. One convict's story I followed at Port Arthur was of a slightly built 20 year old man who was a flax grower from Ireland. He was sent to work in the damp forests felling trees and dragging them to the timber mills, all the time chained at the ankles to other convicts. A number of men were crushed from falling logs causing horrific injuries or death. This poor young man only lasted two years before he died of phenomena from working in one of these chain gangs.

Female convicts were assigned to women's workhouse prisons such as the Cascades Female Factory making blankets, needlework and other articles to raise money for the upkeep of the colony. As there were no cameras in the early years, authorities wrote a physical description to identify the women. 'Front teeth protrude - face slightly pock marked – head flat – chin receding'. It was a confronting read, as if describing cattle at this preserved site.

Quite a number of male and female convicts were also indentured to work for free settlers, clearing farm lands, planting crops or working as servants.

Ten years before the notorious Port Arthur penal colony was built, the Macquarie Harbour penal colony on the west coast was established for the most hardened, unruly, reoffending convicts. One of the cruellest penal settlements in Australia, Sarah Island.

A small, exposed island sitting in the middle of the harbour ravaged by the winds and waves from the Roaring Forties and surrounded by extreme, remote wilderness. Escape was virtually impossible. The convicts were put to work to exploit the nearby, highly valued Huon pine trees for ship building and to supply Hobart town with other building timbers. Bound in chains and heavy irons, often working in waist deep water from sunrise to sunset. Winters would have been bitter in these conditions.

Sarah Island's legacy is filled with mystery and vile stories of inhumane cruelty, malnutrition, brutal floggings, drownings, and even cannibalism. One convict could not face further imprisonment on the island, so he killed another convict knowing he would be executed. This poor soul saw death as his only escape to his horrific life.

Walking through the fragments of various convict sites around Tasmania, you read the maddening stories of the convict's brutal past. Desperately trying to visualise even a glimpse of what life may have been like for these unfortunate convicts was near impossible. Encased in a land halfway round the world from their home with an unknown future of life or death.

Two hundred years after the first convicts landed in Australia, we have shunned the shame of our beginnings and have finally learnt to truly embrace our early convict history. It's even become a badge of honour, holding great bragging rights for those who have come from our early convict stock. I have to admit, I was quite disappointed my own ancestry didn't uncover a convict in our history.

We are now openly proud of our warts and all history to ourselves and the rest of the world. Our convicts rightly deserve their recognition and contribution with building the foundations in parts of our country.

The number of transported and imprisoned convicts began to decrease in the late 1800's as the numbers of free settlers increased. The convict era began to wind down when the mining era in Tasmania began to boom.

Vast amounts of copper, zinc, tin, silver and a host of other minerals were discovered on the west coast, attracting a wave of people to 'seek their fortune'.

***We have finally shunned the shame of our convict beginnings.***

***Our convicts rightfully deserve their recognition and contribution to building our foundation.***

## Finding my first interview on Tasmania's west coast in Strahan...

Arriving in Tasmania I was still clueless how and where to collect stories for my project. It was the beginning of 2016 during a severe bushfire season. Many areas on the west coast and centre were closed to travel, so this sent me in a clockwise direction along the east coast.

Heading south along the coast and visiting the notorious Port Arthur penal colony and other convict sites along the way, I began to absorb more of our rich, yet sad convict history.

By chance, I watched a video in the Information Centre in Geeveston about 'The Piners'. It traced the journey of resourceful tough men who cut the highly prized Huon Pine trees in the remote rainforests in the wild river systems of western Tasmania. The video was set in Strahan on the west coast and somehow I knew this would be the location where I would find my first story. Listening to the regular bushfire updates and rerouting at times, I wandered west, taking in the essence of Tasmania and capturing the magnificent, varied scenery.

Finally reaching the lush, mist shrouded Strahan, I enquired at the Information Centre if there were any of the older Piners still living in the area. I was directed to ask at the local pub. Explaining my purpose once again, the person made a phone call and my first interview was set with a gentleman nicknamed 'Cowboy' for the next day.

A tall figure of a man standing on his veranda greeted me wearing a broad smile. Cowboy absolutely delighted in telling me the story of his colourful heritage and his life as a Piner in the industry's formative period. His grandfather Patrick, was an Irish convict, transported to Australia for seven years. He worked in the gangs in Hobart and managed to escape twice! Each time, he was flogged with 30 strokes by a cat-'o-nine-tails whip and spent 30 days in solitary confinement. He was then sent to the infamous Port Arthur penal settlement for the rest of his sentence. Many freed convicts understandably yearned to create a distance from the social and political system. On Patrick's release, he went 'bush' and began cutting Huon pines in the wild, remote Port Davey area.

Cowboy is highly respected, well known and a third generation Piner. He understood and honed his craft throughout his life. Cowboy still sharpened the saws in the family timber yard at the age of 94 years and loves to keep busy working.

He revelled in retelling me stories of his wood chopping competitions well into his eighties. Chuckling when he would beat young burly men in their twenties.

I was thrilled and honoured to have met Cowboy and shall always remember his joyous laughter and broad warm smile. His stories were a perfect combination of a Tasmanian convict family who helped pioneer an industry with sheer grit.

*Lexa Harpell*

*'It was a hard life,*
*and I would do it all again...'*

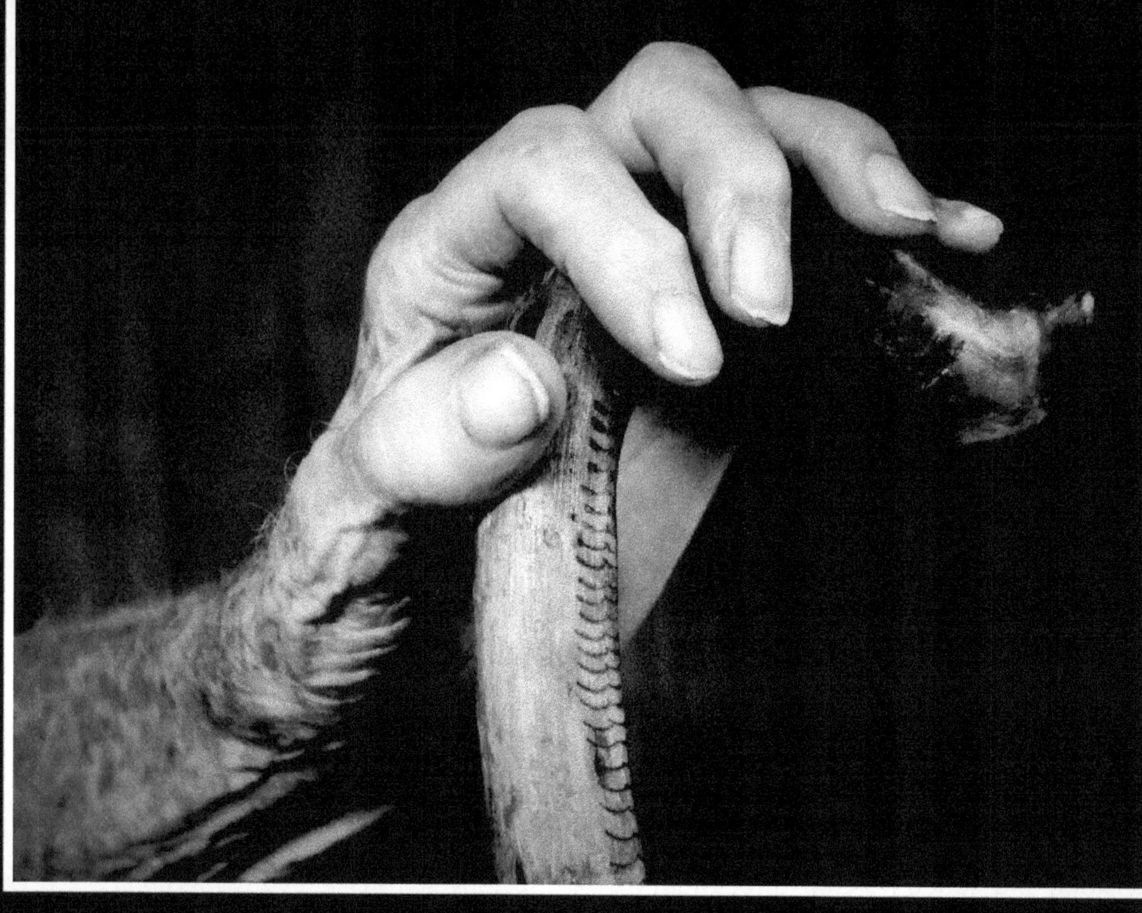

*"It was a hard life, and I would do it all again."*

Every summer we rowed up the river systems through the steep gorges to cut the Huon Pines.

You'd row hard against the rapids until you couldn't row any longer. Then you'd pull the two man punt to the side of the river with ropes, carry the punt and supplies over the rocks and began rowing again. One trip, we had to do that over 70 times. It was hard work.

We were looking for the large straight Huon's. Some could be three thousand years old and could be as wide as a main when felled. Huon's were slow growing and dense. Resistant to rot and insects, the perfect timber for boat building and furniture.

We worked in a small gang for three or more months at a time. We'd build a make-shift hut in the bush. Our food supplies were sacks of flour, tins of jam, tea, sugar and sacks of potatoes. We killed animals in the bush at times for meat.

Once we set up camp, we'd sharpened our axes and cross saws until they were razor sharp, they needed to be. There were lots of trees to cut for the season.

We'd place a flat metal shoe at the front of the felled tree, pin it with chains and use a ratchet around another tree to drag it through the bush and then drop it into the river. Then we'd pin the logs together in the river with chains, ready for the winter rains to float them downstream.

You could have a 100 or more logs chained together in the river. Sometimes you would slip in between the logs, end up in the cold water, trapped. With all those logs above you, you try to find air pockets to breathe and a space to climb back out or you drown.

It was a dangerous job at times and accidents happened. Everything was damp and wet in the gorges. The axe handles would slip in your hands. Men's fingers or hands could be cut off, legs and feet were gouged from misplaced axe hits. Some men feared the cracking sound of the trees falling. You could get trapped under a fallen tree, a few were crushed and died.

You fix up the smaller cuts at camp, but it was a long row back if there was a major injury. One man rowed 48hours straight back to town to get his injured son to a doctor.

I was always good with an axe. I'd sit for hours sharpening my axe with a stone every night, the grinding sound drove my wife crazy. I was still winning wood chopping competitions in my eighties (years). Some of the big young men didn't like that an old man beat them. (Laughing)

*'Piners' were the men who rowed the mighty wild river systems each year in search of the prized Huon Pine trees, for ship building.*

## My journey took me to the west coast's mining town of Rosebery in Tasmania...

Having made some sort of plan, I'd begun to make a list of certain pioneering occupations and the types of people I would like to meet, yet knew I had to be open to possibilities I hadn't considered. Miners in Tasmania was not on my list and I was surprised at the extent of mining and the vast number of minerals found in this state.

In the late 1800's, a rich variety of minerals were being discovered on the west coast of Tasmania, including alluvial and reef gold, silver, copper, iron deposits, zinc and tin to name a few. People flocked to the area to seek work or their fortune. Mining towns and an intricate railway system were constructed, the industry grew rapidly in the boom period. The mine shafts and tunnels were dug and shovelled mainly by hand in the early period.

When the minerals began to dry up, the population quickly diminished. Leaving remnants of ghost towns with large tracks of barren landscapes, resembling an alien planet. Some towns were reclaimed by the forests. The towns of Queenstown, Zeehan, Rosebery and Tullah remain populated with strong evidence of the boom times throughout these towns.

Arriving in Rosebery, I set out enquiring in public establishments, the current mining office and of course the local pub if there were any older miners living in the area. After two days, I turned to the local Post Office and a lady kindly walked me to the home of a gentleman named Geoff who lived in the middle of the town. Geoff and his wife were born and lived in this area for well over eighty years.

He may now be limited in his movements from arthritis in his body, yet his enthusiasm for life had not waned. He proudly showed me a photo of himself in his youth as an amateur boxer. A tall, handsome young man poised in a boxing stance with fists of steel. Strong hands that were well suited for his decades shovelling the ore in the mines. At times, we forget our elderly people were vibrant, energetic youths, this was a good reminder for me to see the life beyond the age.

Geoff explained where a very large lump used to grow on the back of his right hand. The lump was caused by hitting the handle of the shovel to make the shovel dig deeper into the pile of broken ore so he could fill his shovel to the maximum. He slowly began examining his twisted, arthritic hands saying how soft they had become since he stopped working in the mines. The large lump was long gone, but his memories were still very clear.

Geoff was a very proud man – proud of his boxing youth, proud of his daily hard work in the mines, proud of his fitness from his job, proud to have been a miner. Working in such confined spaces didn't suit everyone. Geoff told me some men just didn't last, they were scared of the darkness and the feeling of claustrophobia. However, Geoff loved the lifestyle and odd working hours of a miner and especially the strong mateship amongst the men.

*'The work kept us fit and lean,
no one was over 11 stone.'*

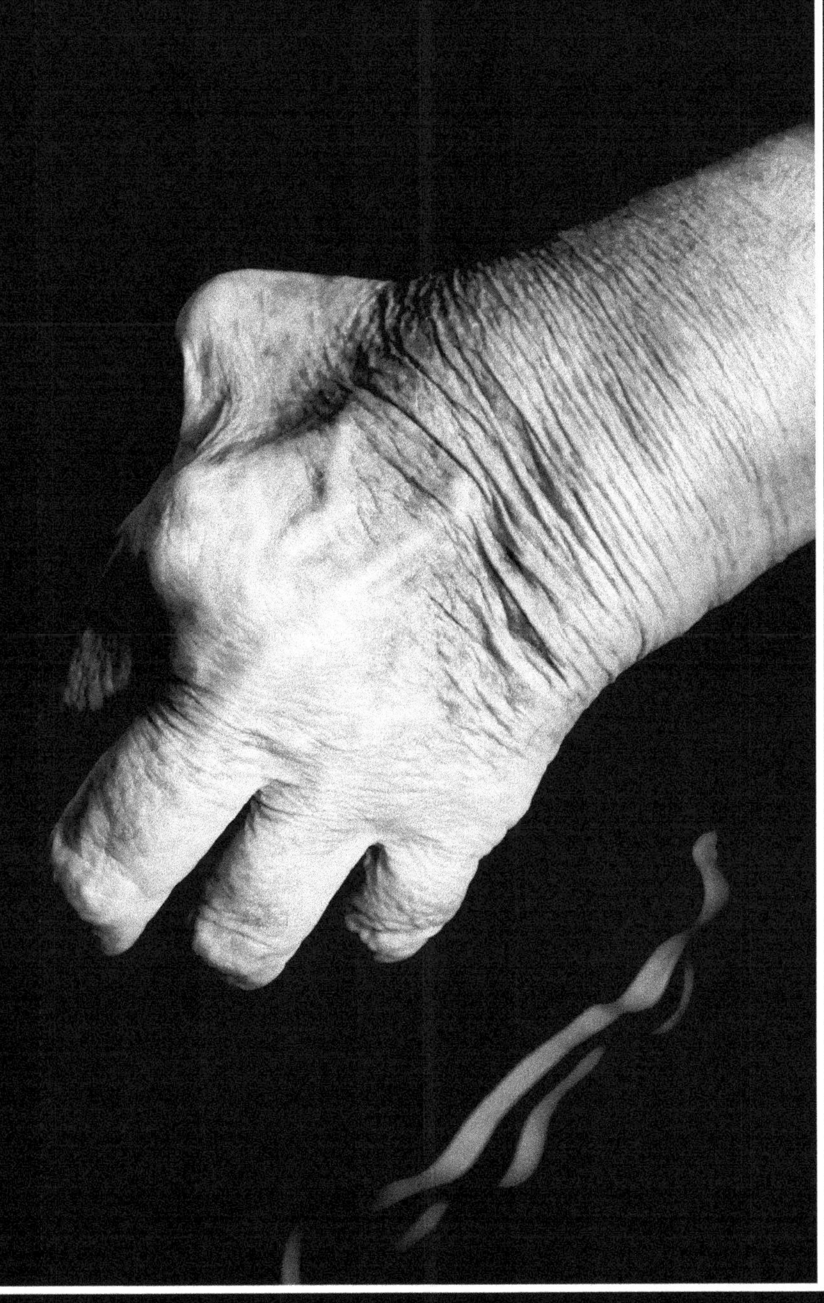

*"The work kept us fit and lean,
no one was over eleven stone back then."*

In my early years I was an amateur boxer. My fists were tough and strong. I guess my hands were suited to the hard physical work that I did over the years working in the mines.

It was always hot underground working in the confined spaces. You wore only a singlet with trousers and boots. The temperature was about the same all year round, day and night. The work kept us fit and lean, no one was over eleven stone back then.

Each day we would enter the darkness of the mine deep underground, wearing a head torch for light. The tunnels were only about seven foot high, just enough to walk through before the opening where our work began. Our hands would need to shovel twenty to twenty five tonnes of broken ore every day.

You pick up your shovel, grip the handle tightly and prepare for the hard jolt digging into the mound of broken ore. I'd used the back of my hand to dig the shovel in deep to fill that shovel. You lift the shovel of ore and swing it across your body into the tipper.

You do this again and again until the tipper was full – around a tonne or more. Then I'd push the tipper about 200mtrs along the train tracks to empty it. You had a bit of a rest pushing the empty tipper on the way back. Then back to shovelling. I'd do this about twenty times a day.

At the end of each day, I'd feel the calloused lump growing on the back of my hand. The callous is long gone, my hands are now soft, stiff and inflamed from arthritis. They served me well over the years.

Working in such confined spaces, you developed strong relationships in the mines with the other men. You looked after each other, that's what mates did. You made sure they were safe and well and you knew they would do the same for you. We needed to be, mines can be dangerous places to work.

I loved the work and life underground. A lot of men couldn't do it, it scared them.

I look at the miners today driving down in big low roof trucks. Their stomachs are so large that they can't even see the truck pedals. In our day, all that shovelling kept us fit, lean and healthy.

*Many brave men labouriously dug a multitude of underground
mines and extracted the ore by hand around Australia,
exposing the country's vast natural mineral wealth.*

## Discovering more in Rosebery...

I was staying at a campsite on the outskirts of Rosebery which was run by the local Lions Club. Tasmania has many free campsites for travellers like myself, especially in small towns. They are usually a bare plot of ground, to park and sleep for a night or two, although some have public toilet amenities. Local communities provide these conveniences with the hope that travellers will purchase petrol, food and goods in the local stores to keep the town's economy alive and allows people to continue to live in their town. It is a win/win for travellers and the towns.

Late in the afternoon, a slightly built elderly gentleman wandered the site asking for donations to the Lions Club for the upkeep of the campsite, which had extra amenities. When this occurs, you naturally give a generous donation to keep these campsites available for everyone who is travelling around our country.

You can learn quite a lot about local history and life when you take the time to talk with our elderly population. I stuck up a conversation with this man named Jack who was well into his 90's. I learnt that he mowed the grass of the whole campsite each week to keep it neat and clean. Jack liked to keep busy and working to keep active.

After learning what it involved to maintain the campsite, the conversation naturally turned to his life.

Jack was born on a farm near Rosebery during The Depression era when money was tight and existing was a hardship. Growing up, he saw his father struggle to make a living with the family farm working seven days a week each year without a break. As with most farms, the sons would eventually take over the family farm and become farmers themselves. Luckily, Jack's older brother showed him another option in life when he began working in the local mines.

I tried to imagine Jack's job working deep in the mines with just a head torch for light in the newly cut tunnels. The responsibility was huge to brace the tunnels with beams of timber to avoid cave-ins. To me, it would be daunting and a heavy weight of responsibility for the lives of fellow miners.

Workers in the mines always worked in pairs in case something happened to one man, then the other could get help or warn others of any danger. It was dangerous work and that created a strong bond between workers, their mates.

Jack was fascinating to spend time with and very generous to share his story. Somehow, I think he was happy that someone was interested to listen to his story. We can't afford to be too busy not to listen to our elderly population's wealth of stories.

'A cave in could kill a lot of my friends
if I didn't do my job right.'

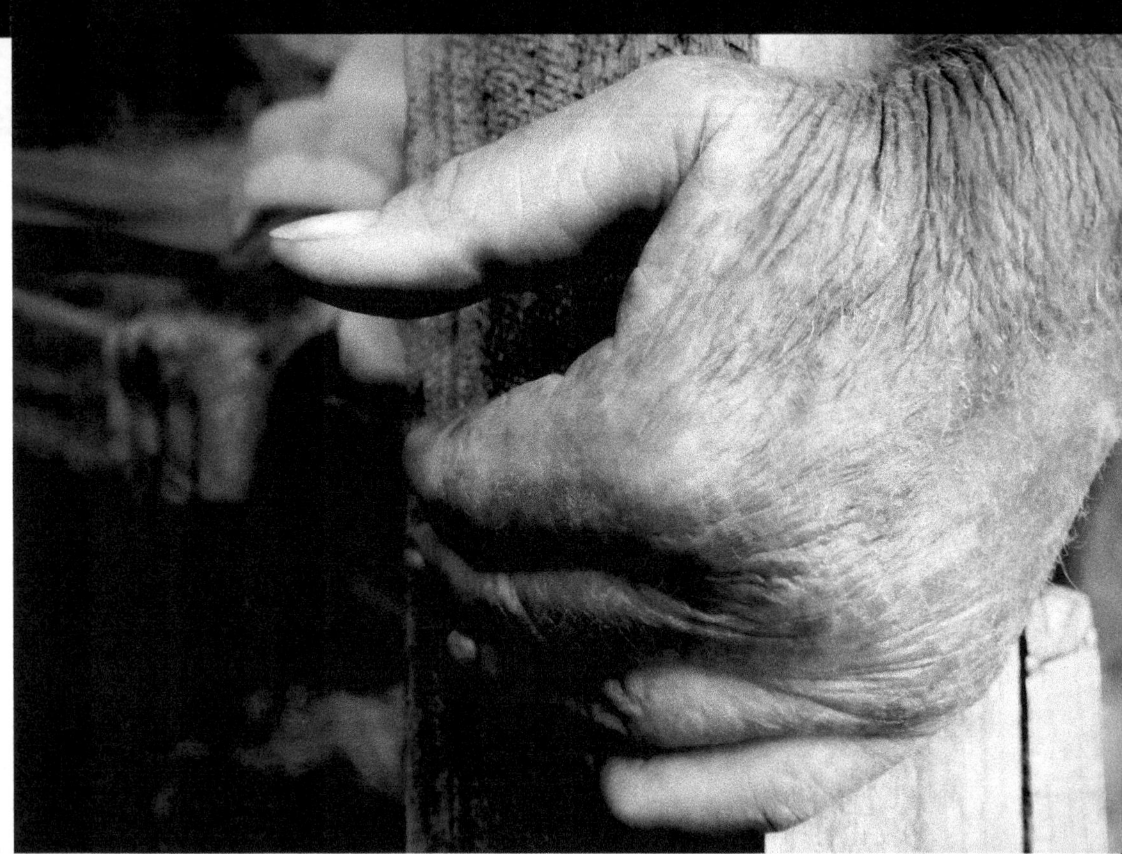

*"A cave in could kill a lot of my friends if I didn't do my job right."*

I was born near this mining town in Tasmania. Our father didn't make much money as a farmer, he was always struggling and worked every day, year in, year out, so I saw no future in farming life. As I grew up, I watched my older brother begin work in the local mines at the age of 15 and he was earning a good, consistent wage. So when I got old enough, I followed my brother and began working in the mines. But I made a decision to also get a trade as a carpenter.

As a carpenter in the mines, your job each day was to pick the cut green timber beams that would brace the mine tunnels. A carpenter is responsible to build the structures to brace the tunnels and shafts of the mine,

You run your fingers over each beam to feel for the strength, straightness or any weaknesses. We can only use the ones that can stand up to the pressure of the mine tunnels and reject the ones that can't.

You carry the caps and verticals down the mine shaft lift a few at a time and then carry them to the newly cut tunnels. You'd always work in pairs in case something happened and the other one could get help. You only had a small head torch, so you feel your way to the end of the freshly cut dark tunnels. We'd look at each beam for height and fit and begin bracing the tunnel with the beams.

We held a lot of responsibility and lives in our hands. We had to keep the tunnels safe for the other workers. Those beams had to brace the rock above us, they needed to hold. So the workers can work deeper into the mines. A cave in would kill a lot of my friends if I didn't do my job right.

The men in the mines were your mates and we all looked out for each other. Trusting each other was very important down there.

I'm glad I made that decision to work in the mines and not a farming life.

Working in the mines was not for everyone. You either loved or hated it.

There was a strong sense of community.

Camaraderie and trust was vital to the safety of all workers.

Your friend's lives were in your hands and everyone understood that.

# Australia's iconic 'Outback'

The Outback screams Australia! The term Outback, The Outback means 'out the back of a town' and doesn't have a specific defined border like a state. Basically, it's used for those widely remote areas with little human population. Generally speaking, it begins in western Queensland/New South Wales, sweeping across Central Australia to Western Australia. Covering a massive 70% of our land-mass, which shows how much of our country is regarded as arid, remote and with little population.

The landscapes are outstandingly dramatic and awe inspiring. It's an iconic part of our country's identity. The Outback is highly impressionable to the world and usually the first vision people have when they hear the word Australia. The vivid red soil which is synonymous with the Outback is due to the high oxide content and one of the most nutrient deficient soils. Every Australian needs to visit the Outback some point in their life to truly understand this country's essence. It's more than you will ever expect.

Naturally, my high excitement rose to experience my first taste of the Outback in North West Queensland. Nothing can prepare you to comprehend the vastness and spirit of the Australian Outback. It is recognised as one of the largest, intact, natural areas on earth.

You know when you have arrived in the Outback, you begin to feel alone, although not lonely. The towns grow less frequent, as do the vehicles and people. The silence is deafening. The enormous vibrant blue sky slaps you in the face demanding to be noticed. The boundless night sky begins to illuminate in utter brilliance and you futilely count the stars until your mind ceases to conceive infinite space. You feel yourself shrink, almost insignificant in the world, space and time. You begin to sense there is more to life than merely existing.

Everything 'out there' is measured with a line of zeros behind irrelevant numbers – apart from rainfall. In some areas, a five year old child may never have seen water fall from the sky. To survive, iconic windmill blades slowly turn drawing bore water from underground aquifers to sustain life to all living creatures.

The Outback is where someone gives you directions and points, 'that's just up the road' - 300 kilometres away. Where you can drive for a day and still be nowhere with colossal rock formations majestically rise out of the earth. Where the world's largest cattle station sits, covering a whopping 24,000 square kilo-metres and you share the land with unfenced cattle stations. Where gigantic walls of red dust roll across the plains engulfing everything in its path and sum-mer temperatures soar well above 40 degrees with no hint of a breeze or shade in sight. It's where the doctor and mail may arrive by an aeroplane and where your nearest neighbour could be 500 kilometres away.

Driving along the relentless straight roads, you seldom see another vehicle. Out of the blue, a monstrous road train thunders by transporting cattle, delivering fuel, food and goods to the remote towns. They are the lifelines for the vast Outback.

You pull over to the side of the road and take a walk. Staring at ongoing stark, barren scenes of commanding landscapes that silences you. You look down and kick the infertile dusty soil which spews on everything in its sight and in silence you wonder. Why would anyone consider to create an existence on this unforgiving landscape?

Our early settlers arrived by horse from the southern states. Slowly driving a mob of cattle and supplies over a distance of a thousand to six thousand kilometres at a dawdling pace of just 15kms a day. It's unfathomable to imagine their blind faith on such an arduous journey into an utterly unfamiliar land. I wondered how many thought of turning back, giving up. Hoping the following day would present water, feed for their animals. Hoping the landscape may change, like the lush lands of their home countries – maybe.

A number of explorers and early settlers perished on their journeys, others fiercely persisted. These early settlers were gutsy, the types of people who were open to adventure and possibilities. They had to possess a resilient, strong sense of themselves to take this immense gamble. They were creating the benchmark for others who followed and unknowingly, they were creating the traits of our unique identity. There was no guarantee of success, all they could do was 'give it a go'.

Long journeys through the Outback were greatly applauded by our nation because we understood the odds were stacked against the people. To the point when a jury acquitted Harry Redford for stealing 1,000 head of cattle from Bowen Downs Station, near Muttaburra, Outback Queensland.

Harry was a stockman at the cattle station in 1870. Realising the station was over 200miles long and could not be regularly monitored, he began to build stockyards in the remotest area of the station. Gradually, he herded 1,000 head of cattle into the stockyards, then along with just two other men, they drove the cattle to South Australia. Harry sold the mob at Blanchewater Station near Marree for a staggering £5,000.

What was so astonishing and greatly admired by the jury and even the judge, was that the journey took three months over 1,300kms and through the infamous Strzelecki Desert. Just ten years earlier, explorers Bourke and Wills had perished in their attempt through this desert. The Outback is about people's endeavours and *that* is what we celebrate.

After many months of travelling in these remote areas, glimpses flashed through my mind as to why people created a life against these unforgiving odds in a most inhospitable land imaginable. One day I woke, sensing its all compelling beauty and understood the why.

The Outback humbles you where words cease to have meaning. The vast space creates a sense of personal freedom devoid of limitations, where you must rely on yourself and totally respect nature – or perish. It constantly pulls you, forces you to make that connection.

***Life in the Outback ultimately becomes a profound relationship between you and the land.***

## Learning just how harsh life was in the Outback, Julia Creek, Queensland...

Driving in Outback Queensland, I heard about the annual aptly named, Dirt and Dust Festival on the local radio station. This would be a must see and visit. Julia Creek has a rich proud history as a vital gateway for the livestock industry. For me, this was an iconic image of an Outback town. My thoughts of Julia Creek in two words would be remote and flat. With barely a tree in sight, your eyes take in the vastness and that iconic red dirt veils everything in sight.

It wasn't too difficult to find someone to interview in this relatively small town during the activity of the festival. Enquiring in the local pub and various establishments, the name 'Pat' was consistently mentioned. Someone put me in contact with Pat and his wife Betty and I was welcomed in true Outback style, open and friendly.

Pat and Betty were both in their late 80's years and both were born in Outback Queensland. Living most of their amazing life in and around Julia Creek. Listening to Pat's story unfold, it took all my might not to let my jaw drop to the table while picturing him as a nine year old boy sleeping on a blanket alone each night in the remote Outback. My head was swirling with images of snakes and rogue wild animals that could harm or kill him, let alone protecting the valuable horses. Curiosity got the better of me, so I casually asked Pat if he carried a gun (for protection). He titled his head slightly to the side and said "What would I need a gun for?" I casually replied, "Just asking." Instantly feeling naïve and stupid for asking the question. It made me think about how much knowledge, strength and resilience people had to possess from a very early age to survive in this harsh environment.

Betty's story hit my heart with a thud. Most children during this era began work life at an early age. Yet they had moments of nurturing and affection from their parents or knew their parents were teaching them skills for their future. From what I understood, at the age of four, Betty was orphaned and taken in by a woman merely to work on her farm with seemingly little consideration towards her well-being and nurturing. Betty's reflective approach about her life stunned me. She said that she didn't know her parents, so she didn't know if her life would have been better or worse. The profound, honest simplicity was humbling. That acceptance to what life dishes up to you kept emerging with this generation. Nowadays, we tend to fixate on our childhood issues, creating excuses for ourselves, it made me wonder why and how did it change.

Pat was extremely proud of his daughter and repeatedly insisted that I visit her at their cattle station in the Northern Territory. I wanted to honour and respect his wishes, so three months later I found myself driving through the gates of the cattle station in the Top End.

Pat's daughter had been expecting me and greeted me warmly. Fifteen minutes into our conversation I learnt Pat had passed away just a few days after I had met him. I choked up and became a blubbering mess, desperately trying to take breaths as a flood of tears rolled down my face. It took a while to compose myself to finally speak my words of condolences. Wondering why it had such a deep effect on me. I learnt that Pat had only just begun to share his stories of his life in the past year. I realised the importance it was to meet this beautiful couple and hear these snippets of our history. I felt honoured that he shared his story with me and ultimately you.

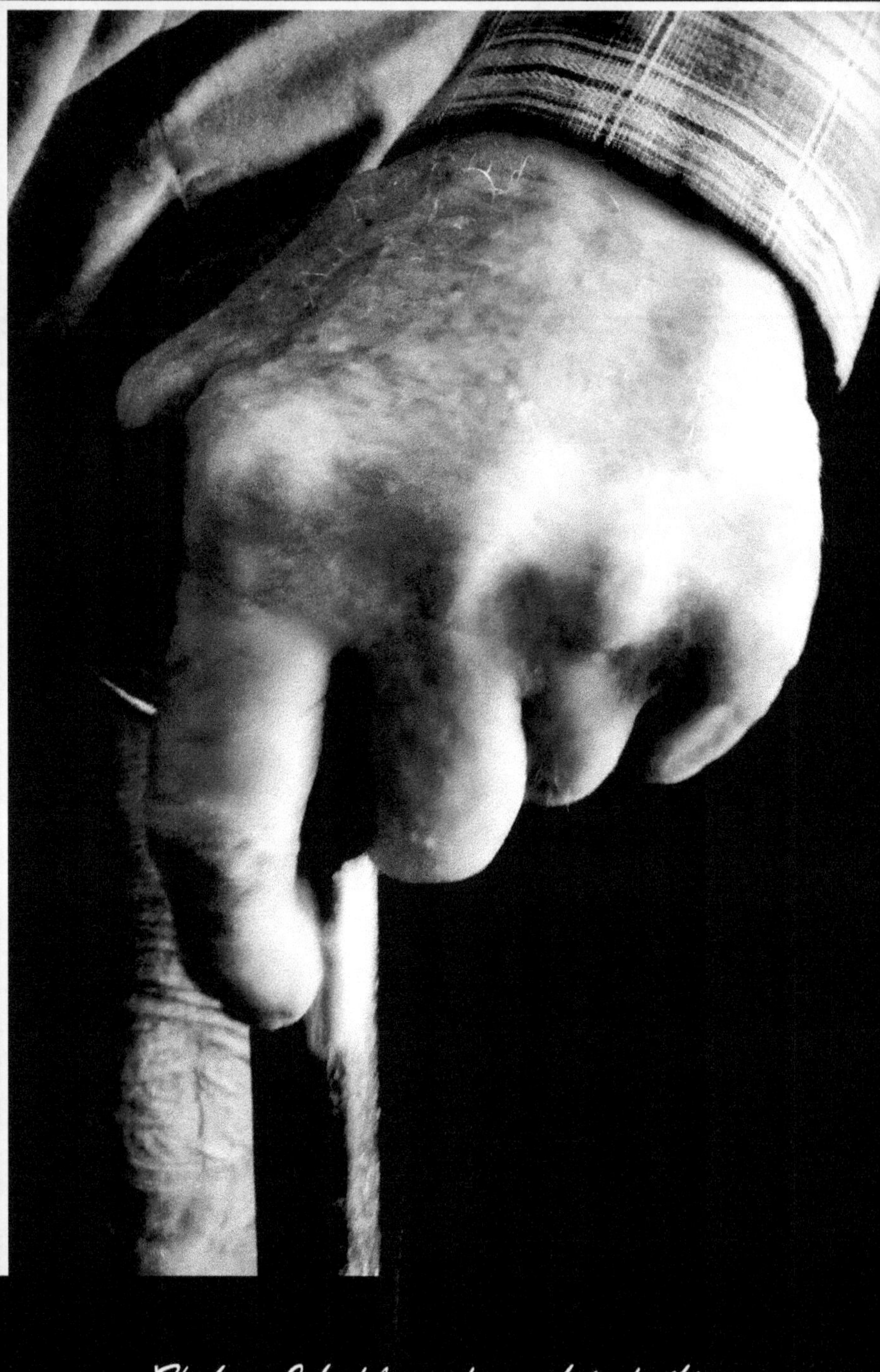

*'He knew I had learned enough to do this onmy own..*
*I was just nine years old...'*

*"He knew I had learned enough to do this on my own and dad trusted me. I was just nine years old."*

As a kid, we moved around a lot in the Outback around Winton and Cloncurry. Dad was a Drover, a Team Driver, a Brumby Runner. I was one of six children. Once a week dad would take one of us boys to help him work and to learn the ways of the Outback and his jobs. I was already riding horses by the age of five.

When I was eight years old, I had my first job as a roustabout at a sheep station. I skirted and picked the dags from the wool. It was only seasonal work and I was always the youngest worker in the (shearing) shed.

Dad woke me up one morning and gave me a hand drawn map and twenty five horses. I had to take the horses to Julia Creek, 100 miles away. He knew I had learned enough to do this on my own and trusted me. I was just nine years old.

The map showed where I could water and graze the horses each day. I hobbled the horses at night and slept on a blanket. Mum gave me some 'tucker', a piece of corned mutton and some bread. The salted meat had to be wrapped in wet hessian each day so it wouldn't go off. A sandwich a day was enough and I drank water from the creeks. It took me five and a half days to deliver the horses and then I rode back home. I rode this track about twice a month delivering horses to Julia Creek until I was 14 years old.

A little later, I also began to move 500 head of cattle 4-5 times a year to Boulia which took five to six days. I was the youngest drover around Julia Creek. Dad had taught me lots of skills over the years and I learnt a lot from watching him work.

I never knew what money was, I didn't have any use for it. My bag was always filled with tucker, that's all I needed. The first payment I got for my work was when I turned 17. Dad gave me £25 to buy a new saddle, I still have it. When I close my eyes, I can still remember the smell of the leather from that first day.

When the war broke out, I joined the army for six years, and when I returned home I began work reconstructing the railway line here in the Outback. Later I worked at the saleyards, drafting, sorting cattle and trucking them out of Julia Creek. Occasionally I bought a few weaners for myself and was soon able to buy a little block of 10,000 acres for my first cattle station, then another block of 39,000 acres. I sold this block for a good price years later, enough to buy our small family farm of 63,000 acres. We had to dig the dams and trenches for all the water pipes to water the stock and to the house.

*Many children from this era grew up quickly, taking on adult responsibilities and roles at a very young age.*

*'I never knew my mother and father, so I don't know if my life would have been better or worse...'*

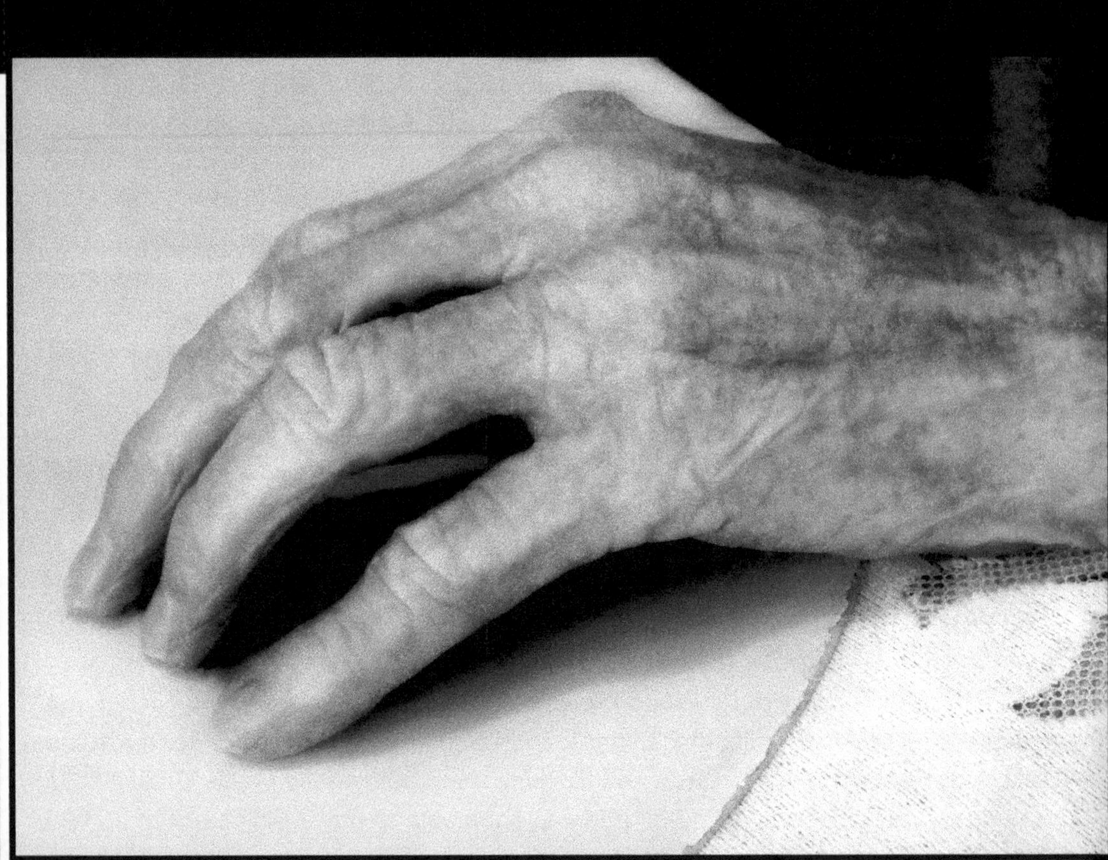

*"I never knew my mother and father, so I don't know if my life would have been better or worse."*

I was orphaned and taken in by a woman when I was four years old to live with her on a dairy farm. She made me work straight away milking the cows.

I only had one dress, which I wore every day, it was just an old onion bag. I didn't have any shoes. It was so cold during winter that I had to put my feet into the fresh cow paddies (cow manure) to warm my feet, for a while at least.

Every day I had to bring in the 'milkers' (cows) from the paddock to the shed for milking. There were about 200 or more cows depending on the year. Sitting on my wooden stool, I would have to (hand) milk cows from 7pm to 6am every day of the week.

When I got a little older and with so much practice at milking, I was able to milk 12 cows an hour by hand and strip them for cream. The quicker I became, my milking hours grew shorter, but I got more jobs to do around the farm.

When I wasn't milking the cows, I fed the pigs and calves. There was always house work. Cleaning and washing, and the silverware always had to be polished.

Once a week I would take 30-50 cows to the sale yards in town on my pony.

I had little time for anything else. No schooling, so I never learned to read or write. I would have liked to have learned to read and write.

The lady wasn't the kindest of people and I was nervous or scared of her when I was young. She had a lot of large varicose veins on her legs. When one of her veins burst, she would yell at me to 'fix it'. I had to run to the house to fetch a penny (coin) and a bandage and then jump into the pond to let the leaches attach to my own legs. I placed the leaches on her burst vein to suck out the excess blood. Then I placed the penny on top of the vein for pressure and I had to wrap her leg with the bandage. That happened many, many times.

I'd thought about running away a lot of times. By the time I was 15 years old, I was fed up with the way I was treated by the old woman. I had enough of that life. So one day I took my pony and left. I didn't have any money, but I managed somehow.

I later met and married a kind hearted cattleman and we built a good life together working and eventually owning a cattle station. I still regret that I didn't learn to read and write.

*The profound acceptance of life's circumstances kept emerging from this collection of people.*

## A long shot meeting in Julia Creek...

After listening to Pat's story, I wondered if there were any women who had been drovers. It was a pie in the sky thought and seemed a bit of a long shot, but I just had to ask around the town again. As I was enquiring to staff in the Post Office, a lady standing next to me spoke up and told me her mother-in-law would be ideal to interview and gave me her phone number.

Making the phone call, I spoke to Beryl who was quite happy to meet the next day. Beryl was a lively, highly spirited lady who was 85 plus years of age. She had an effervescent joy for life and spoke rather quickly. Laughingly, quite a few times I had to ask Beryl to slow down as my pen and thoughts could not keep up with the speed of her conversation.

Beryl was born and lived her life in various parts of the Outback and the Top End of Australia. She was also the first white child to live in remote Tennant Creek in the Northern Territory.

Like most of us, I'd never given a lot of thought about how our roads were originally created. It was people like Beryl's family who had to clear and carve the land at some point, usually with just a pick and shovel.

Today, we (including myself) whine about so many minor things, what we don't have and what we want. For Beryl there was only the barest of necessities. For a generous part of her life, home was a basic, transportable *Bow Shed. Schools were non-existent in these remote places, so she educated herself. Her first pair of shoes was when she was fourteen years old. She also began working alongside of her father from a very young age.

Beryl's reflective words still burn in my mind. "Life is what you make it. No one was worse off than anyone else. I didn't think it was more difficult, there are lots of things you can do without in life." Before this trip, when I wanted water, I'd turn on a tap, for electricity was just a flick of a switch and I'd shop without regard if I 'needed' my purchases. Now I had to monitor my power, water, purchases on a daily basis. Living was minimal, confined and inconvenient at times. Yet in comparison to Beryl's early life, I was still living in relative luxury and had absolutely no reason to complain.

Contemplating this story over the following days, I vowed to stop whingeing to myself for the absence of life's modern conveniences. Changing my focus to fully appreciate what I was gaining rather than lacking. In essence, I was merely exchanging a handful of comforts for incredible life experiences, learning and creating a life that was worth living. Yes Beryl, there are a lot of 'things' you can do without in life!

At the end of our conversation, Beryl told me that she often missed the simpler life of her youth. I was slowly beginning to understand why.

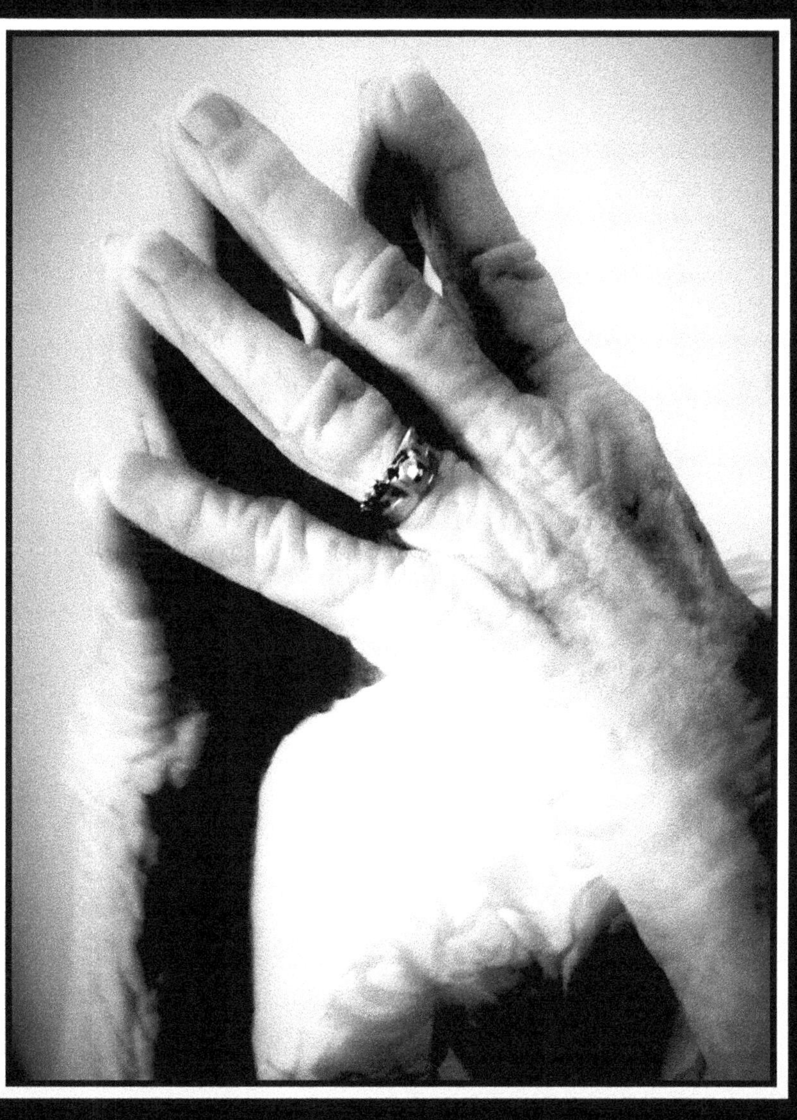

*'The hardest road we built was from Wyndhamd to Halls Creek, about 250 miles.*

*"The hardest road we built was from Wyndham to Halls Creek about 250 miles."*

I grew up in the Top End, and was the first white child who lived in Tennant Creek.

We were always moving. Dad worked making the roads up here by hand. Dad would build a Bow Shed for the family to live under while he worked. Then pack up and move the Bow Shed on the horses to another location every week or so. It was the only way to keep the family together while he worked

We would collect water from creeks using an old kerosene tin and collect wood for the cooking fire. I taught myself schooling living on the roads.

I was the eldest child, so I helped dad build the roads from a young age. The hardest road we built was from Wyndham to Halls Creek in Western Australia, about 250 miles. All cleared, dug and cut by pick and shovel.

Dad had other jobs on cattle stations in between building roads. I helped him dig holes for fencing and feed the barbed wire through the posts. I went on my first muster when I was nine years old. I was on a horse from the age of three.

We ate bread and dripping quite a lot. Dad would buy us children a large tin of condensed milk every six months. Each Sunday we could eat a spoonful. It had to last, that was our treat. We didn't have toys or celebrate Christmas. I didn't own a pair of shoes until I was fourteen years old.

Life is what you make it. No one was worse off than anyone else. I didn't think it was more difficult, there are lots of things you can do without in life.

I eventually left home and married a Drover. Our first home was another darn Bow Shed!

We would move two mobs of either cattle and calves or bullocks each month to Kajabbi trucking station. About 800-900 head of cattle each mob. The cattle could only walk about 10 miles each day.

I had four children under the age of five years and our children came on the droves. I carried our 10 month old baby daughter on my horse. The boys rode their own horses and we slept in swags.

Our food was better than when I was a child. I cooked each night for the family and the 8-10 stockmen and stockwomen. Tea (dinner) was curry and rice. With no refrigeration I carried corn salted meat wrapped in wet hessian bags. Breakfast was fritters and left over curry. I didn't eat vegetables, still don't like or eat them. I made dampers and scones with homemade jam. Butter was carried in tins with a wet rag wrapped around it, or stuck it in mud to keep it cool. We did get to eat fresh meat once we arrived at the trucking station.

*Women in the Outback had an equally tough life In some areas, more so than men.*

# Our love affair with Drovers

Droving is romantically entrenched in our identity as portrayed in many of our ballads, poems and songs. Drovers and their teams were the lifeblood of the livestock industry around the country. From the lush green plains of our southern states, the mountains of our High Country to the searing heat of the Outback. Our drovers etched their place in our history and deep in our hearts.

Learning and understanding the different terminology of this industry took a while and it altered from state to state. I was quickly corrected at times when I used the incorrect wording! Fingers crossed I have it correct here.

The reality, it wasn't always a dreamy romantically built life as most of us envision. The responsibilities were huge and the conditions were often cruel. A drover's life was constantly on the move, isolating, with plenty of time to think. Many drovers, stockmen and cattlemen penned emotionally moving bush poetry and ballads about this transient, lonely life as part of their legacy to our heritage. In saying so, I guess whose perspective we are looking at would make a huge difference in our view if it was a 'dreamy' lifestyle.

Indeed, a rare breed of people. Robust, independent, life's loners. Some didn't marry, others left their families for months or years at a time to fend for themselves while they drove mobs of cattle to market or new pastures. In ways, they were 'absent' from society. They valued their freedom and space regardless of the pitfalls and dangers. It appeared this deep love came from a basic human sense to be at one with nature.

Drovers were independent contractors who were in charge and responsible to move stock from cattle stations to market, to another cattle station or to search for water and feed during times of droughts or seasons. Stockmen and stockwomen, jackaroos, cattlemen worked under the direction of the head drover.

The Head Drover had to be a tough person who knew how to handle large mobs of cattle as well as their workers. They were in charge of delivering the stock, organising their team of stockmen/cattlemen and a cook. They organised the working plant and night horses, working dogs, food, cooking gear and other items for the journey. Their payment was based on the number of 'head' (of livestock) delivered in good condition and within a certain time frame.

A mob (number of livestock) could be a few hundred to several thousand 'head' and the length of the drive could be from a week up to two years or more. Drovers who opened up new country were called Overlanders and travelled over exceptionally long distances.

Their attention to the mob was around the clock. Keeping them on the move, fed and watered during the day and keeping them calm and settled during the night.

The men took turns at being the 'ringer', who rode around the mob to keep them in a tight group. A 'rush' could begin when something would spook the mob and the team would have to bring them back together and calm them again. Sometimes men would be crushed or die as they slept under the many hooves during a 'rush'.

Injuries also occurred when chasing breakaways through the scrub, trying to dodge low branches or encountering rogue bulls. There were numerous dangers that experienced drovers and stockmen had to avoid when moving large numbers of cattle, including moving stock across swollen rivers where drownings occurred.

Recently, research has been presented about a number of Aboriginal stockwomen who also contributed to the pastoral industry in the Outback, dating as far back as the 1860's. The information relates to the 'frontier wars' between our Aboriginal people and European conflicts where many men were killed. The cattle stations had to continue somehow, so a number of Aboriginal women took up the demanding, traditional men's work as stockwomen on several cattle stations. In the early years, it was illegal to employ women as stock people, so these women had to dress like men.

One woman from the 1950's named Maudie Moore was renowned as one of the best stock people in the Kimberly region. "Maudie Moore, jumping off a horse, grabbing a bull, swinging him down, cutting off his horns, tagging his tail and jumping back on the horse — and she was in her late 50s — these were hard, strong, women of that time." **information from Tauri Simone's research.*

There are many epic livestock drives recorded in our history. The longest recorded journey was over 6,000 kilometres from southern New South Wales, through Central Australia to the Kimberly region in 1883. More recently, in 2014 Tom Brinkworth bought 18,000 head of cattle in the Top End during one of Australia's severe droughts. The cattle were trucked to Winton in Queensland, then split into nine mobs to be walked along the inland stock routes to southern NSW.

It was an ambitious two year journey using some of the best drovers, stockmen and stockwomen in our country. The cattle drive honoured Australia's long tradition of droving, keeping the 'romance' in our heritage alive.

***Drovers are romantically entrenched in our heritage.***
***This time honoured tradition will always live in our hearts.***

## Meeting an old time drover in Camooweal, Outback Queensland...

I had my sights on meeting an original style of drover of the Outback. The ones who lived and breathed their time honoured craft throughout their life.

Rumbling along in my campervan near the border of Queensland and Northern Territory, I noticed a small road side sign 'Camooweal Drover's Camp'. Surely someone there could connect me with an older drover. Within a few minutes, I pulled up outside of the museum in the small dusty town of Camooweal.

Large pictures and stories of well-known past drovers covered the walls. There was a familiarity to each image, as if I somehow knew them. Their heavily browned and highly weathered faces were chiselled with deep furrows from the effects of a lifetime of exposure to the harsh sun and punishing elements. Their broad smiles radiated with sheer joy and their multi crinkled eyes ignited life.

The gentleman made a phone call and told me he could take me to meet with a well-known drover who lived in Camooweal. We drove just a few streets away and pulled up outside a home. As we walked through the gate, Pic appeared wearing his well-worn, wide brimmed hat, a light denim shirt and a red kerchief tied around his neck. Pic looked ready to move a mob of cattle with his saddle and gear sitting in the front yard.

Pic was in his late eighties and an old school style Head Drover through and through. Moving cattle in the Outback was his life. I became mesmerised by Pic's stories and by the specifics of life and the responsibilities as a Head Drover. He showed me his old metal water cans, weathered saddle and sleeping rugs as he explained the finer details of being a drover. During my time with Pic, I easily slipped in and out with the romanticism of the idea of being a drover in the Outback.

It would be a hard, lonely life at times, yet I could see it would be highly fulfilling for those who had a great love of nature and adventure. I began to see droving as a chosen lifestyle rather than merely a job. Yet the reality was you had to be very tough, living hard every day and night, pitting yourself against nature on a daily basis.

Constantly exposed to the harsh sun, dust storms and torrential rains. Continually breathing in the dust kicked up from the cattle's movements and preparing for a host of encountered dangers. Moving the mobs safely across flooded rivers, chasing runaways and keeping them calm. Their thoughts were constantly on the mob's welfare to lead them to water and feed each day. Keeping them calm and in good condition until their work was done – at delivery.

Later that night, my thoughts went back to the pictures on the wall in the museum. Yes, I did know those faces. They were our visions of drovers we grew up with, as portrayed in our folklore. Australia's romantic love affair of a life filled with adventure, freedom and a strong connection to the land.

*Lexa Harpell*

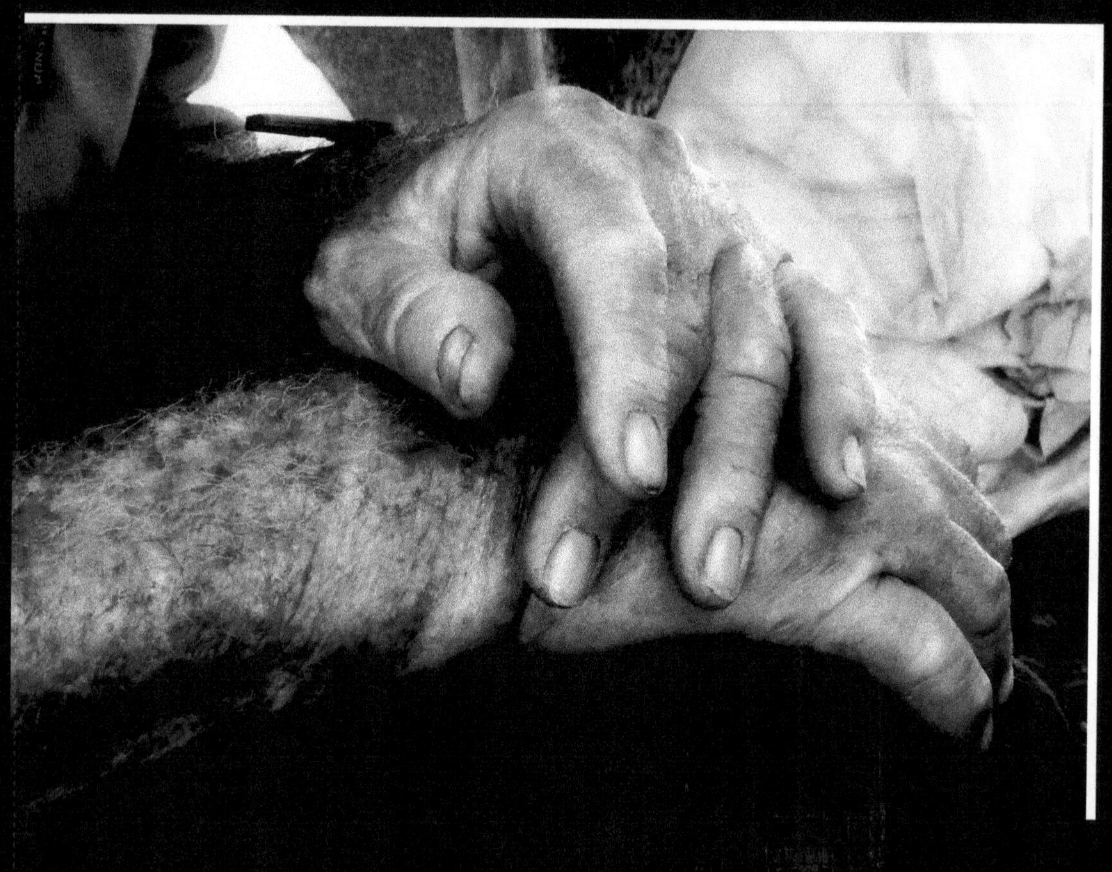

*'We nurtured them, kept them calm to delivery.*
*The old ways are lost...'*

*"We nurtured them, kept them calm to delivery.*
*The old ways are lost."*

As a Drover, the most cattle I moved in one year was 18,000 head. The longest was around 2,000 miles and took us 28 weeks and 3 days, moving 12,500 head of cattle to Walgett with just three good stockmen and a few Jackaroos.

Eight week trips was the usual here in the Outback. At times you would need to swim the stock through flooded rivers. Our horses never stopped working, you needed to look after them well.

Sometimes you started out with eight men and finish the drove with three. You have a head stockman an off sider and about 16 Aboriginal Jackaroos.

You had to be well prepared and planned. With 45 plant horses and 8 pack horses for food supplies. And a (horse) shoeing pack, the horses would often lose their shoes.

One horse carried a beef pack of corned salted beef. Others had 4 packs of flour, ½ bag sugar, tea, jam, treacle tins. Each man carried their own water bag.

By day, you have the head stockman at the front of the mob and two men turning them at the sides.

At night, a Ringer would ride around the mob, you would rotate (the men) every 2-3 hours riding around to keep the cattle settled in one place. Stock whips were important to keep the cattle in line.

Most cattle station managers have no idea how to handle cattle now. They don't rest the cattle properly. We nurtured the cattle, they were settled and calm by the time they arrived at the station. We always filled the cattle (with food and water) so they could settle for the night.

We were grown men at the age of 15 or 16 years. All stockmen back then wore high heeled RM Williams boots with spurs. You always carried a revolver on the leg to shoot cleanskin bulls. We were always on the move, that's the life of a drover.

*Somehow I don't think the traditional ways will be*
*totally lost, especially in remote areas.*
*In times of drought, drovers can still walk their cattle along*
*our famous stock routes dotted around the country.*

# The Top End - untamed, timeless and exhilarating

The naming of the first established eastern states of Australia was in a British tone. New South Wales, Victoria, Queensland. At one point we must have decided to ditch the airs and graces and in true Australian form, make it effective, simple and 'call it like it is'!

So we used compass points and directions. 'South' Australia, 'Western' Australia, 'Northern' Territory. So the Top End is exactly where you would think it should be, at the top end of Australia.

The name may sound rather simplistic, however this area is far from being simple, it's complex, raw and excites all your senses. Add an element of danger to make it thoroughly exhilarating! (*This account will include The Kimberly region which joins to the left of this area as they share similar characteristics.*)

Undoubtedly I was very excited to experience this northern most region. I guess I saw it as an untamed, untouched frontier. I'll admit I was a little uneasy to be travelling on my own through this remote area. This was mainly through my own ignorance, yet my reservations were eased the more knowledge I gained.

Travelling through the dry flat plains of the Outback, the landscape begins to change as you travel north into the tropical monsoon climate of the Top End in the Northern Territory and Kimberly region.

An ancient, timeless land, you feel its presence in absolute awe. Nature's colour palette broadens and intensifies. It holds immense tracks of extreme, raw wilderness holding some of the oldest and most spectacular rock formations on the planet. The most famous site is the remarkable Kakadu National Park. It's also home to the largest display of ancient Aboriginal rock art, some are estimated around 50,000 years old.

There are two distinct seasons known as The Wet and The Dry and it is consistently hot throughout the year. Around 1,200mm of rain relentlessly falls during The Wet, flooding the extensive river systems which snake their way across the lands. This rainfall creates brilliantly coloured floodplains, billabongs. The rain also fills the almighty gorges and canyons creating pristine waterholes and majestic waterfalls.

So what makes it exhilarating? An element of danger to remind you we are mere visitors and Mother Nature is in charge of this land. Australia is well known for its deadly creatures, add the deadliest of all to this area, the highly aggressive salt water crocodiles.

They are opportunistic predators who are acutely aware of their surrounds and can sense and smell 'food' over long distances. The reality of the danger set in when you begin to see the numerous 'Warning Crocodiles' signs and hear a good number of horrifying crocodile fatalities from the locals. So I set about to learn as much as I could about their environments, movements and came up with a strategy. I decided not to go near any kind of water unless it came out of a tap!

A number of early explorers perished or failed in their attempts to reach this area by overland. Setting out from the southern states they had to traverse through deserts and contend with droughts. Water is the most precious commodity on this continent and when there is no water to be found, stock and people die.

In the late 1800's, the government opened millions of acres of pastoral leases in the Kimberly region to those who dared to take this ambitious overland journey. It was to 'push' the livestock industry outwards across the country into these remote regions. A colossal gamble with potential future rewards for those who dared. Some tried, some failed, only a handful succeeded. Men died along the way from either malaria, accidents and a few even took their own lives, unable to endure the unbearable conditions of the journeys.

The longest, recorded overland cattle drive in Australia began in 1883. Two families set out from Goulburn, NSW with 670 head of cattle, two supply wagons pulled by a bullock team and 60 horses. Three years and 6,000kms later, they arrived in the Kimberley region where they established their new cattle station, Fossil Downs. More than half of the cattle and horses died along the way as did some of the men.

This was an epic achievement, newsworthy to spread across the land! Journalists *had* to know the details of their journey, but the MacDonald brothers kept declining to share their story and experiences. Eventually the brothers were offered a hefty £500 to tell their story. Reportedly, they responded "It was worth that much to forget the trip." It must have been an utterly savage journey. The sacrifice and cost to human life and livestock was high to establish this industry in this timeless, remote region.

Another epic journey began in central Queensland to the Kimberly region in 1882 with 800 head of cattle and 200 horses. Covering 3,600 kilometres and taking just under two years. Around 300 men were employed at various times over the duration. Yet only four completed the whole length of the journey. All four were just young boys, two Aboriginal and two European. The youngest being just fourteen years old. You could only imagine by the time they completed the journey, they would have become men in every sense of the word.

***It is complex, raw and excites all your senses.***
***Mother Nature reminds you 'she' is in charge of this land. – respect or perish.***

## A long search rewarded me in Mataranka, Northern Territory...

Travelling through the Outback, many station owners and drovers spoke of the Aboriginal stockmen/cattlemen with high regard. Saying some were smarter and more skilled than many of the head drovers and they greatly depended on them. The Aboriginal stockmen and cattlemen were pivotal to the success of the cattle industry in the Outback and northern regions of Australia. Naturally, I was very keen to hear some of their stories.

It was becoming rather difficult to find someone who moved cattle into the Kimberly and Top End. It was also difficult to find someone to fit the age group I was looking for. Travelling through the Northern Territory I asked in many places with no success. I persisted over several months. I'll admit, I was continually distracted exploring and photographing the incredible wonders of the untamed, raw landscapes which delayed my efforts.

Eventually learning that cattlemen in this area generally had a lower life expectancy, mainly due to the extreme harsh conditions and constant dangers. So I decided to disregard the age group in this instance and seek someone who worked the ways of the earlier cattlemen.

Visiting yet another cattle station asking if they knew where I could speak with an older, generational Aboriginal cattleman. I was told, 'try in Mataranka'.

Enquiring at the Community Centre, a lady straight away said "I know the perfect person". We walked across the street and wandered around the park until she found a gentleman named Roger. She explained to Roger what I was doing and he graciously agreed to tell me his story.

We sat in the park for hours under the shade of a large tree listening to Roger's captivating stories as a cattleman in the dangerous Top End and Kimberly regions.

Roger spoke in a soft casual voice as he rattled off a long list of cattle stations he worked for throughout his life. He was deeply proud of his skills, knowledge and the fact he was a third generation cattleman. His sheer love for his job seeped through all his spoken words and expressive hand gestures. Yes, I believed he was born to be a cattleman.

During our meeting, I found myself slightly mesmerised how Roger's hands moved with slow, rhythmic movements as he spoke. His hands were telling the story. When Roger voiced, 'my favourite place is home, I was born here - Mataranka', the back of his hand gently and lovingly brushed the ground. An eerie shiver shot through my body in that moment, as if sensing Roger's strong connection to his home and this land. A moment I will cherish and not forget.

*'I'm a Cattleman,*
*I was born to do this...'*

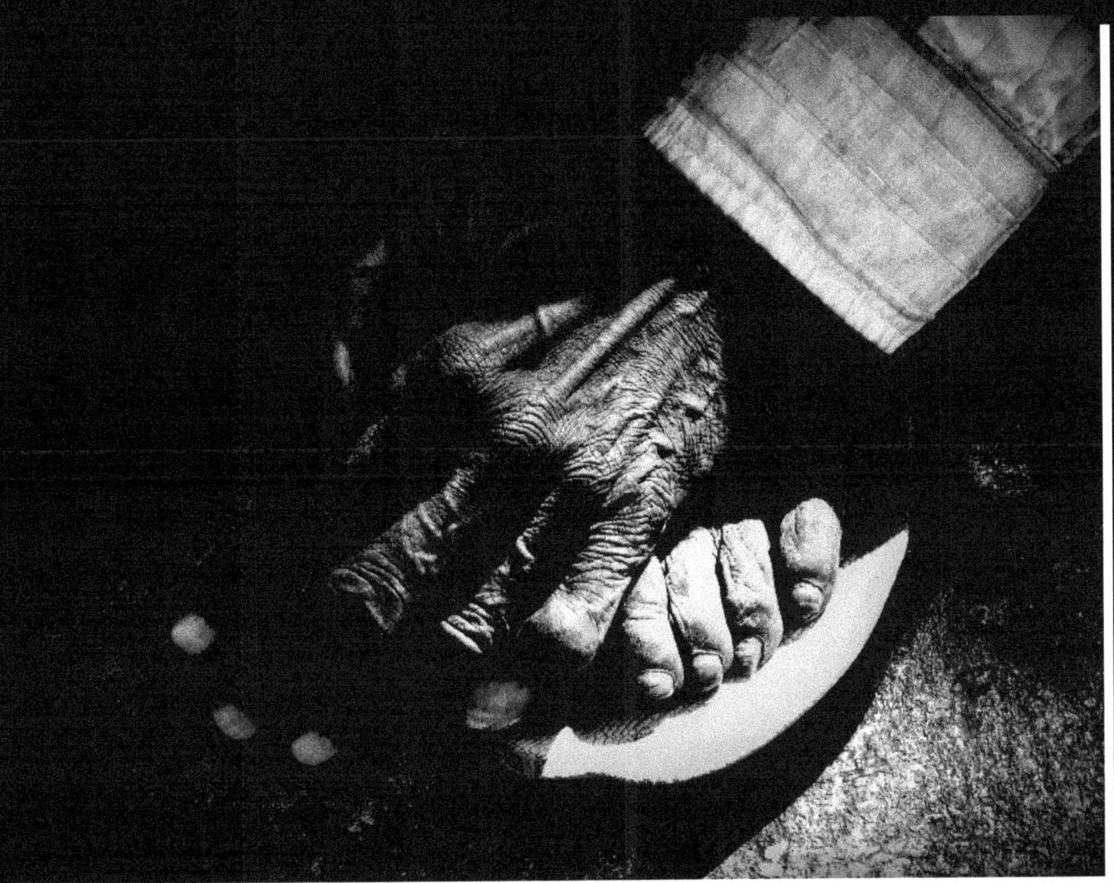

## *"I am a Cattleman – I was born to do this."*

My grandfather and father were cattlemen, it's in my blood. I was born to do this. I'm proud to be a Cattleman, it's my game, my trade, my life.

I worked for a lot of cattle stations around here, in the Northern Territory, Kununurra, the Kimberley's. I began working when I was 11 (years old), I was a quick learner and good at my job. I could ride any horse, even the wild Brumbies, but you had to always be careful with the wild horses at the beginning, breaking them in (laughing).

My day began at 4am, breakfast was at 8am. I worked 13 or more hours a day. I was a good cattleman, many people wanted me to work for them. Lots of stations around here.

I moved stock around, big mobs (of cattle). To dry land before the wet season, to market, Shorthorn and Brahmas. I was a bull catcher, I caught wild Brumbies and trained them. Mustering camps. I branded stock, fixed fences, cut trees to make new fence posts, mustered cattle, burnt grasses to clear the stock yards, there was always work to do, it never stopped.

I had to look out for crocodiles, wild buffalo, wild boars and dingos out there, in the bush. It's a hard land up here, a hard job, a dangerous job, a good job.

There was no time to marry or have children, travelled around too much. I was always moving to somewhere all my life.

My favourite place is home, I was born here, (gently stroking the ground) Mataranka.

*Aboriginal stockmen, stockwomen and cattlemen played a vital role to the success of the cattle industry the in Outback, and still do in some areas. They innately knew the land, they understood the animals and were quick to learn the many skills required. Even though horses were not part of the natural landscape, these men and women instinctively knew how to ride.*

## Meeting a 'friend' in Mataranka, Northern Territory...

When my time with Roger naturally came to an end after many hours, he told me to speak with his friend Jeffery who was also a third generation cattleman. They worked together many times throughout their lives. Roger pointed towards Jeffery who was sitting under a large shaded tree and I walked over and met his friend. Obviously, I explained why I was speaking with Roger and asked if he would like to share his stories also. He was quite willing to share his time with me and tell his story as a cattleman.

It was fascinating to hear a different side to this somewhat perilous job. Jeffery shared more of the details and the dangers they encountered on a daily basis. As with all the stories, I hung on to every word in an effort to somehow place myself 'in their shoes' both visually and emotionally. Desperately grasping fragments of understanding of a life I had not experienced.

Visons of an intense sun scorching your eyes and skin all day long. Continually breathing in volumes of dust kicked up by the cattle and horses. Grains of dirt flying into your eyes. Broken branches ripping into your flesh as you chase runaways through the scrub. Broken bones, concussion when kicked by horse hooves as they were being broken in. Terrifying encounters with crocodiles, rogue bulls and water buffalo. You would certainly develop an exceptional high level of awareness and lightening reflexes to survive this job in this region. Not a job for the faint hearted.

Jeffery's face lit up when he told me that he thoroughly loved mustering cattle most of all in his job. Then telling me he lost the sight in one eye from a broken branch while riding hard through the scrub rounding up the cattle. I guess it is all part of the acceptance of the highs and lows of the job. Scars they would wear proudly.

Jeffery told me the younger generation have little interest in learning the cattleman's traditional ways, they want short cuts. Suddenly, I felt a heavy sadness. A generational lifetime of knowledge and skills Jeffery and other older cattlemen could impart to the next generation is slowly disappearing.

During my time in this region, some locals took me deep into the bush by 4WD where they made their own tracks through grasses that were well over a metre high. This was land where cattlemen drove their mobs through the bush, along dark silent rivers, glorious billabongs ablaze in colour and a place where crocodiles call home.

I managed to see quite a few crocodiles warming their bodies on the bank of the rivers and their slide marks in the mud. The most chilling was seeing a few closely watching us from the waters with just a small portion of their heads eerily exposed. I kept quite close to the vehicle despite the local's reassurance. These exhilarating trips gave me just a small view of the dangerous, yet stunningly beautiful landscape where the cattlemen would move their mobs of cattle each season.

'It's a dangerous jib,
you have to watch your back all the time...'

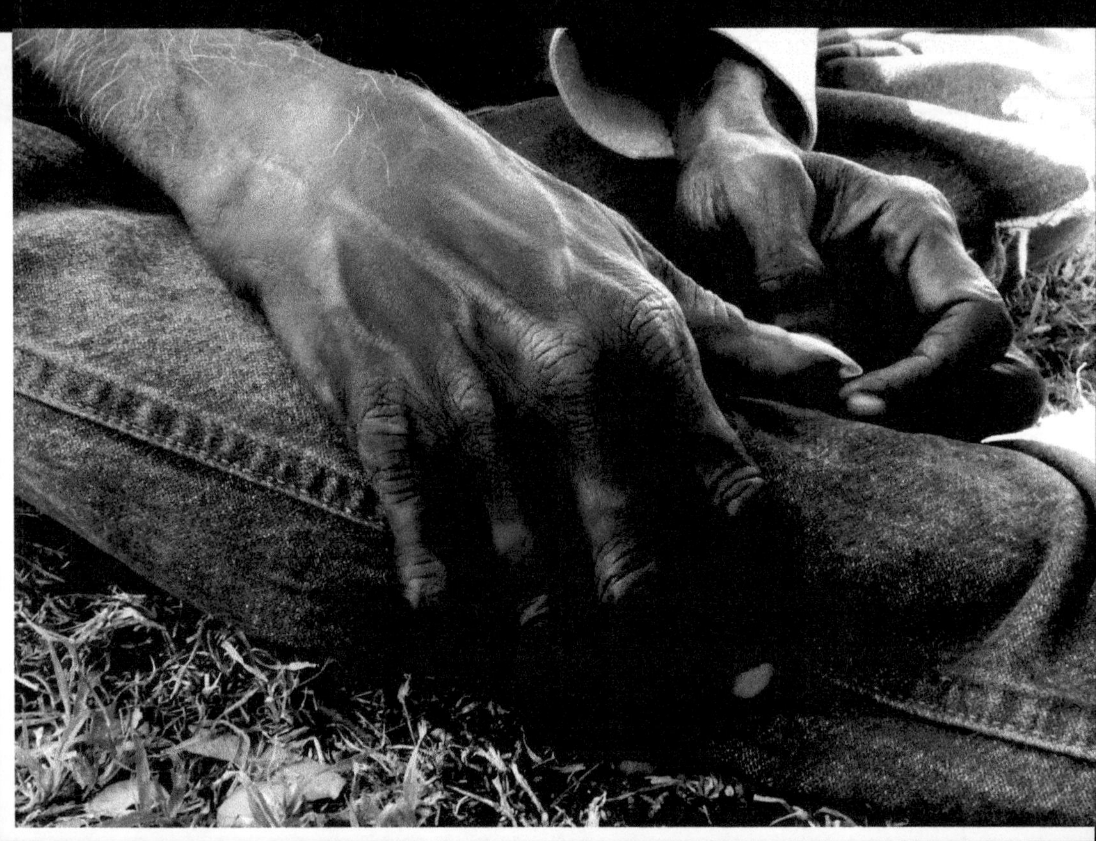

***"It's a dangerous job, you have to watch your back all the time. Crocodiles are always after your stock."***

By the age of 16, I was ready to take a job as a cattleman, it's what I knew. I am a third generation cattleman.

I loved mustering cattle through the scrub, you have to be very fast at times and it can be dangerous. I'm blinded in one eye from hitting a tree branch. My grandfather was killed by a Shorthorn bull.

Cattle always had to be moved up here. Moved from the wetlands to dry land each year and back again when The Wet was over. You need to find and move them to food (new pastures) when the land dried up in The Dry.

You'd move 1,000 head of cattle, with just a few good men. You chase the break-aways through the scrub and bring them back to the mob. It took a few days to settle them on the move. At night two men at a time would ride in a circle around the mob to keep them together, all through the night.

The stock needed water daily. Spending weeks in the bush at a time up here, you were always asking yourself "Water, where is it?" You had to be careful because the crocs (crocodiles) lived in the rivers, creeks and billabongs, waiting, waiting for food. They could smell you and the stock long before you arrive at the water, and they were ready.

You don't see them much by day, but you can see their eyes at night when you shine a torch in the water, but not all of them. They are fast, the stock has no chance when a croc gets one. Sometimes you would have to shoot the croc to protect your stock. You are always watching, looking for their tracks. I'd look for Bush Tucker of wild bananas and wild honey in the bush when I was moving stock.

The day's work was long and constant. When we weren't moving stock, we would catch wild Brumbies to train as stock horses. You could catch 3-4 a day and it would take 4 weeks to break them in and quiet them down. You would need two men all the time to do this work, it's very dangerous.

The dry scrub and grasses in the yards needed to be burnt at the end of The Wet to stop bush fires during The Dry. It also makes new grass to grow for the cattle's feed. Fences always needed repairing and stock yards needed to be built. You learnt to plait cow hide for your stock whips. There is always something to do.

You train youngsters to become cattlemen, although there are fewer now who want to do this job; our way, the old way. They want to muster on bikes, they don't seem to want to learn the way of the land and animals anymore.

*The harsh conditions and constant dangers took its toll on many cattlemen.*
*It's about the love of the role and a deep respect for the land.*

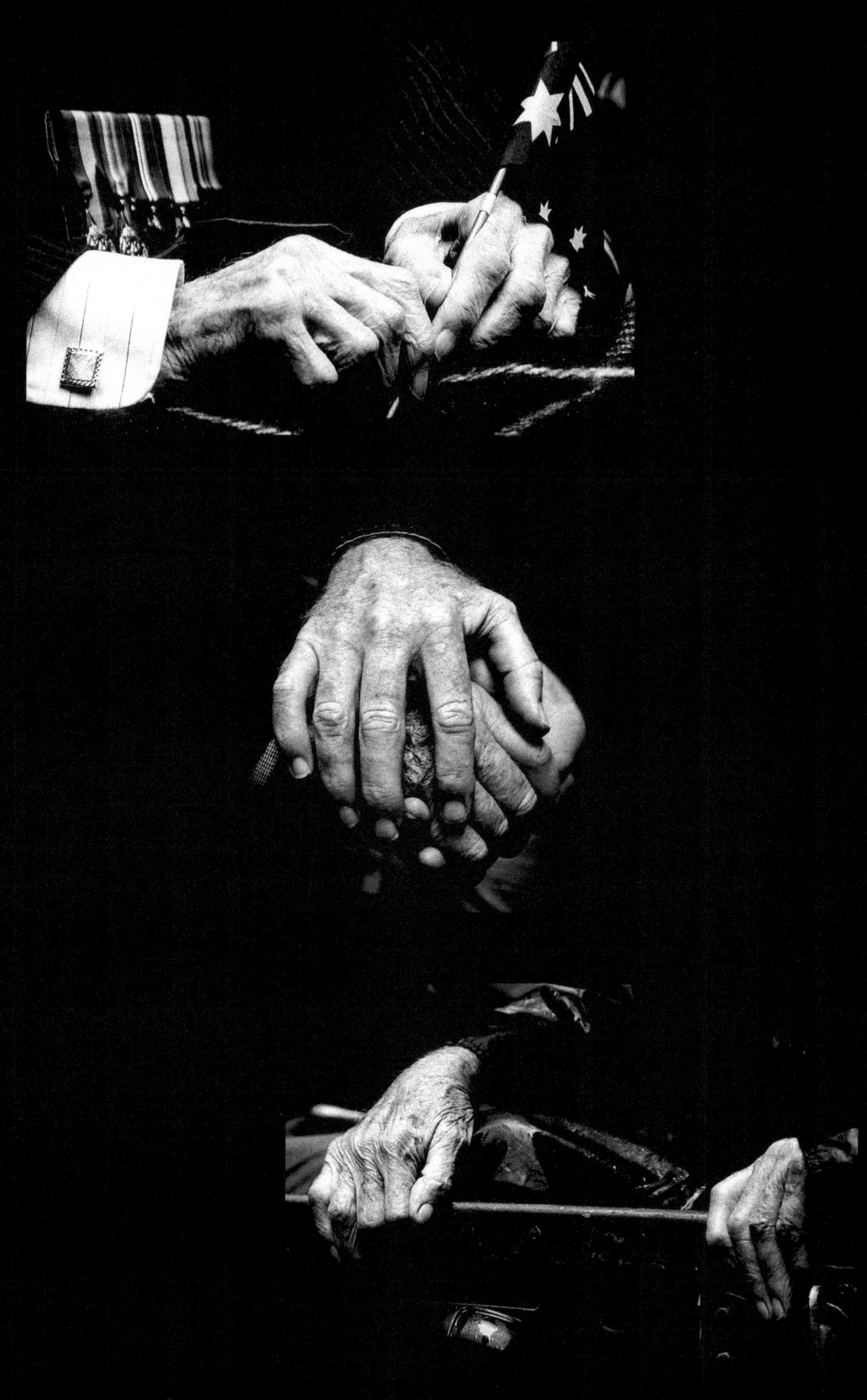

# Our Defenders

*"Stories of deeds accomplished by Diggers, the capturing of dug-outs,
the rushing of machine-gun positions are spoken of,
but as the Australian is one of the most modest of men,
many stories of desperate deeds and high enterprise will never be known
beyond the limits of camp and the field of war."*

The above exert is from Irish soldier, journalist and novelist Patrick MacGill's book, The Diggers. Describing the Australian soldier's well-earned reputation during WWI. The Anzac legend was born and formed from many pivotal campaigns. That same reputation has continued with our defenders of our country.

Those early traits of our identity created spirited, tenacious and courageous fighters. Taking on challenges against great odds. Their ingenuity and ability to adapt and do things differently served them well in times of war. Their celebrated humour and underlying modesty pushed them through the tough times. Mateship was their creed, their bond like no other.

**Mates - Mateship** was embodied deeply during times of war. Mateship is more than friendship. It is a silent, intense bond of a shared experience amidst the toughest conditions. It's an unspoken and unconditional support for each other.

Our convicts termed the word to look out for each other in their dark circumstances. The term was also strongly used by early settlers and gold field diggers for the same reason. Mateship is still in our culture, calling on our 'mates' in times of hardship, help and even business associations.

Whether we agree with war or not, paying homage to the many men and women who put their lives on the line for future generations is the least we can do today. Anzac Day isn't about celebrating or glorifying war, it's a solemn day to remember those who defended our country and values with their precious lives. A gift for the lifestyle we live today.

Just before I embarked on this journey, I attended an Anzac Day dawn service in my hometown, Bondi. It was the year of the 100$^{th}$ Gallipoli anniversary and one the most powerful and moving services I've ever attended. As the dawn light barely began to illuminate the blue waters and golden sands of Bondi Beach, we were asked to turn towards the ocean and picture the moment our Anzacs began to land on a similar beach, 100 years ago, Anzac Cove. The pressure of the silence was intense, mixed with stifled emotions from all as we strained to visualise that utterly tragic landing.

As the service finished, the mood slowly changed as the beach began to come to life with movement and sound. Surfers entered the water to catch some waves, people jogged along the shore and children running towards the waves in laughter. Walking along these golden sands I thought, this is what they defended, our values, our way of life. It made me wonder, how different would our life in Australia be if our defenders didn't 'do their job'?

Many men and women participated in World War I and World War II in some way. Men of age joined the forces to fight overseas and within Australia. Too many young teenagers lied about their age to enlist to 'do their bit'. Women joined to work as nurses to mend the wounded amidst the fighting.

Others who were not of age or valued in specific jobs stayed to look after the factories and the nation's food supply. Women had to step up and fill the vacant men's jobs in many areas across the country.

The ones who returned home after the war, picked up the pieces of their life, went back to their jobs, found new work or struggled with life. Many believed their job was done and they preserved their country and values. They continued with life again and in true style of this generation, moved on in silence.

They mostly didn't talk about the darker side of the war, they kept their nightmares to themselves. Many didn't talk about it at all. My own father always refused to talk about his years in WWII. To him, it was over, finished, end of discussion – silence.

The following quotes came from chance random conversations from our older defenders around Australia. I recorded these words I'd heard in local pubs, RSL Clubs and Anzac Day services from men who were summing up their thoughts of WWII.

The images were captured on a rainy Anzac Day in Sydney where their hands were poised proudly in remembrance.

## OUR DEFENDERS THOUGHTS/MEMORIES

"We did our duty for our country and the Commonwealth, it was expected."

"We didn't want our country to change, so we fought to keep it that way."

"We were told to fight, to protect our country, but we fought overseas."

"We were an unruly lot, but we were mates and achieved
our objectives in spite of what others thought we could do."

"The British couldn't work us out, us Aussies were fierce fighters."

"We were the first to put our hands up to hold the lines and hold them we did."

"We came out of nowhere, they (the enemy) didn't expect what we would do."

"We knew what had to be done and we just bloody well did it."

"Quite a few of us lied about our age to join the war."

"I was a big country boy who could shoot really well,
if only they knew I was only fourteen years old."

"Those young inexperienced boys became men after their first battle,
they grew up pretty quick, they had no choice."

"They knocked me back three times just because I was too young,
the fourth time I just told them I was eighteen."

"You had good mates who fought with you side by side, they could save your life."

"Mateship was very important, it kept us together."

"You needed mates, good mates to survive those horrors."

"You would put your own life on the line to save your mates."

"I felt blood and death; too many times, way too many times."

"Hand to hand combat is not pretty, you feel the horrors of taking someone's life."

"There were a lot of sacrifices made by good men to keep our country ours."

"Too many good men died, far too many."

"I held two friends in my arms as they died, it was
a bloody shame, a real bloody shame."

"We lived in terrible conditions for years."

"The trenches were filled with death, you'd wonder when it would be your turn."

"War was a 24 hour a day job, with no time off."

"I was sending mortars to kill people I didn't know, they were soldiers
just like us doing their duty for their own country."

"It was supposed to be an adventure, we were naïve."

"We thought of our loved ones back home often; it kept us going."

"Sometimes you'd cry a little reading those letters from home,
wishing you were there. But if we didn't do our job here,
there wouldn't be a there."

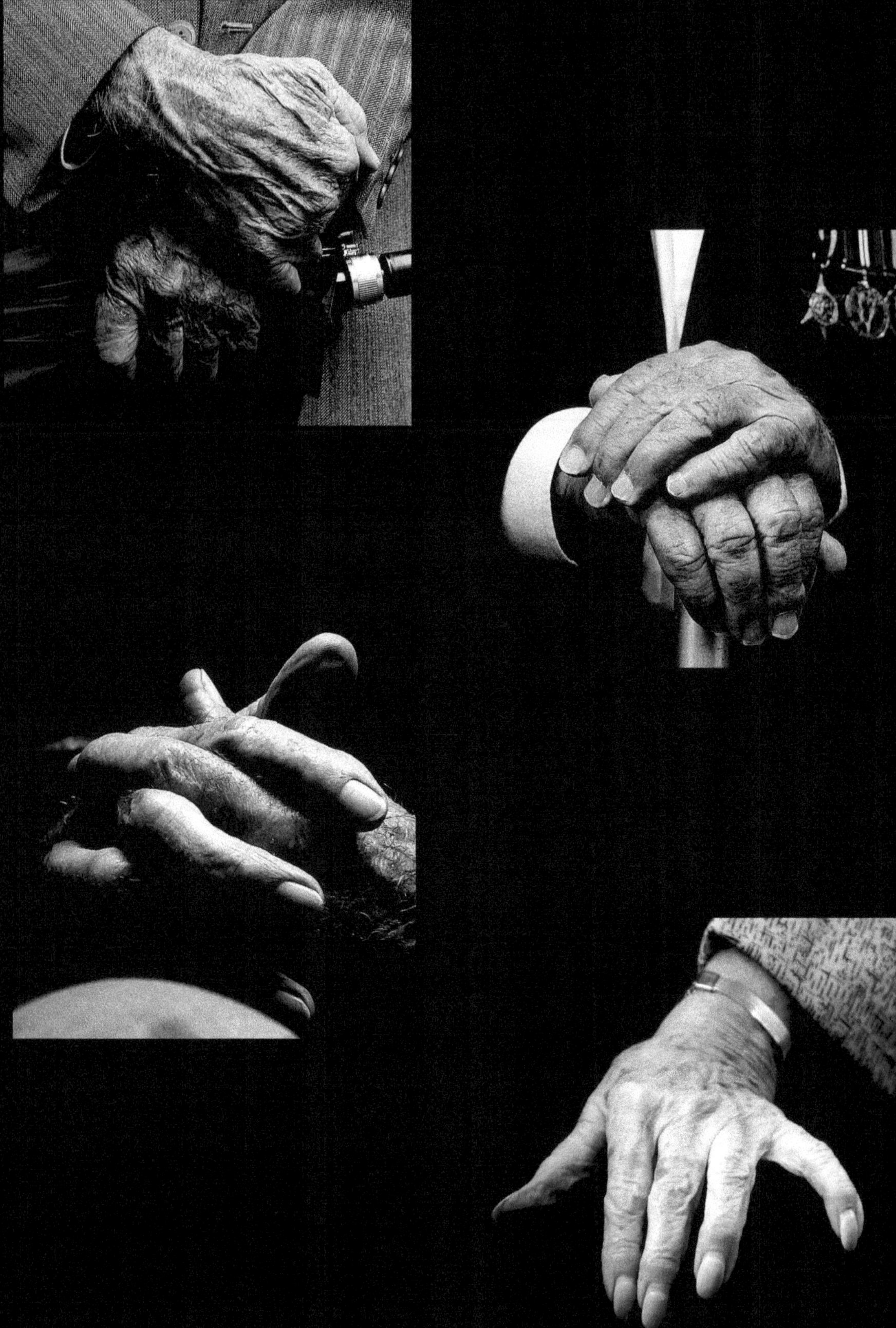

# Riding high on the sheep's back

Images of a full fleece Merino ram became a strong identity to Australia's prosperity. Our association with sheep was strongly ingrained in our culture and invoked a deep pride.

We had strong visual reminders with a ram's head was proudly minted on our Shilling coin. Later appearing on our two dollar note, one dollar and fifty cent coins in our decimal currency.

The Australian sheep industry inspired many to pay homage to this great pastoral success. **Banjo Patterson**'s iconic bush ballad and song – 'Waltzing Matilda' and 'Clancy of the Overflow'. **Tom Roberts**' noted oil paintings – 'Shearing the Rams' and 'The Golden Fleece'. The lively, classic children's song, 'Click Goes the Shears' also drew attention to our unique developed slang.

As kids, we excitedly watched sheep shearing events in awe and given treasured pieces of oily raw wool at the Royal East Show each year. Many Australian's grew up on the much anticipated traditional Sunday roast leg of lamb.

Australia's prosperity rode high 'on the sheep's back' (referring to wool sales) for almost 200 years, yet it was a lot of hard work and high ingenuity by many to create that success.

Right off the bat, the 'colony' (Australia) had to quickly learn to sustain itself financially and economically. In the early days, there was a lot of trial and error to find out what animals and breeds could flourish on this strange new land. Sheep adjusted and were bred for meat and wool. Farmers began to breed different types of sheep to suit Australia's diverse climate and geographical areas. Yet one breed stood out with great success.

In 1797, twenty six sheep from the Royal Spanish Merino bloodline arrived in New South Wales and carefully bred for their wool. Rising to the challenge, Australian farmers began further selective Merino breeding which would later yield ten times more fleece with a far superior fibre than the original Spanish Merinos. Within just four decades, Australia became the biggest wool producer with some of the finest and most sought after wool in the world.

By 1890 Australia was home to over 100 million sheep. Just a few years later, Australia suffered a brutally savage drought, wiping out almost half the sheep numbers. It took farmers twenty years to regain prior stock numbers. Later, Australia reached its peak with a whopping 175 million sheep. Wool became Australia's dominant export with great pride. Our economy grew strong from sales of our sheep's wool and meat around the world.

Hmmm - Now, all those sheep needed to be sheared at least once a year!

Strong, able bodied men travelled by horse or foot from station to station to shear the tens of millions of sheep across the country. Shearing was a demanding, hard, physical job, unnaturally bent over at the hips all day clipping the wool from the sheep took its toll on many men's backs.

There was always friendly completion in the shearing sheds across the nation for who could shear the most sheep in a single working day to be 'crowned' the 'Gun Shearer' in the shearing shed. In 1892 at Alice Downs station in Queensland, Jackie Howe set a new weekly record, shearing a staggering 1,437 sheep in a working week of 44 hours and 30 minutes. Jackie became an Aussie legend when egged on by his fellow shearers to break the national daily shearing records.

Jackie was a powerfully built man with large hands and strong wrists. He accepted the challenge and sheared an astounding 321 sheep in one working day which was around double the average shearer's numbers. A record that has never been broken using the simple blade shears of the period. Many shearers at the time wore a navy blue singlet as it gave more freedom to move their arms and body. Apparently Jackie was wearing a navy blue singlet on the day he broke the daily record and the singlet became known as 'The Jackie Howe'. Still today, this style of singlet has become a 'uniform' of sorts for trade workers across our country.

Our sheep industry's success became a symbol of independence and growth. Australia could proudly stand on a world stage from its well-earned efforts of high ingenuity against the odds. Australia was no longer being viewed as just a convict colony, rather a country of prosperity and possibilities. The Merino became an iconic symbol of wealth to Australians as we 'rode high on the sheep's back'!

With the introduction of synthetic fibres our wool industry took a bit of a decline. Although we still have about 100 million sheep and our wool is regarded as the finest and in demand across the globe. Actually depending on the year, we are neck and neck for the title with our friendly rivals 'across the pond', New Zealand. But neither of us like to admit being second to the other in any year!

***Australia could proudly stand on the world stage.***
***We were now seen as a country of prosperity.***

## A dual surprise in Quirindi, New South Wales...

When you reach a town, you explain your brief to people in the community regarding the type of person you are looking to hopefully meet. In small towns people generally know everyone and their background. Their suggestions are mostly spot on, however they generally don't reveal the person's background, just the person's name with 'I know the person to speak to'. You quickly learn to trust their judgement.

Hearing each person's personal story unfold was always an incredible surprise for me. This time, I received an additional, unexpected surprise.

One of the locals of Quirindi, set up a meeting for me with a lady named Millie who was 90 plus years old. I was to meet her in the local museum.

Arriving at the museum, I began looking for what I thought a lady in her nineties might look like. OK, we are all guilty to having pre conceived ideas at some point, this was one of my moments. A diminutive, stylishly dressed lady wearing blue jeans, a leather jacket and 3 inch heeled boots greeted me and introduced herself as Millie. It took me a few seconds to shake my notion of a lady in this age group 'should' look like! I smiled and thought 'Never assume...this is going to be an interesting meeting.'

Standing at just five feet tall, Millie had a soft, quiet strength about her. We found a discreet place to sit in the museum and I listened to her story unfold.

Although I met Millie in Quirindi, her story revolved around Werris Creek in NSW. Werris Creek became a gateway on the Great Northern Road for Drovers to water their mobs of livestock at a waterhole near the creek. They would then continue to head north or northwest into the Outback from the eastern states of Australia.

Werris Creek began as a mixed pastoral area in the mid 1800's, mostly of Merino sheep and cattle. Like Tasmania, convicts were used on the early pastoral stations as part of the labour force to clear the land and build structures with backbreaking work to grow the foundation for the industry

Millie's story made me think about inner strength, vitality, and a strong sense of responsibility. There was little difficulty visualising Millie as a small, wiry, energetic child who followed her adored father each day as he worked. She told me she was not the kind of person you'd find at home cooking and baking as you'd imagine many young girls would have done from this era,

A station hand's role was physically demanding even for some men, yet this petite young girl had no hesitation taking on a man's job for her family to survive. It didn't sound as if Millie thought it was a great burden. She loved the outdoors, physical work and knew every detail of her father's job. But it was still a man's job, and Millie was merely a young, petite girl.

Those qualities of people from this era kept emerging. Doing what it takes, tackling anything and taking on the hard challenges to survive.

*'I guess in a way, I was learning my father's job, for that eventful day...'*

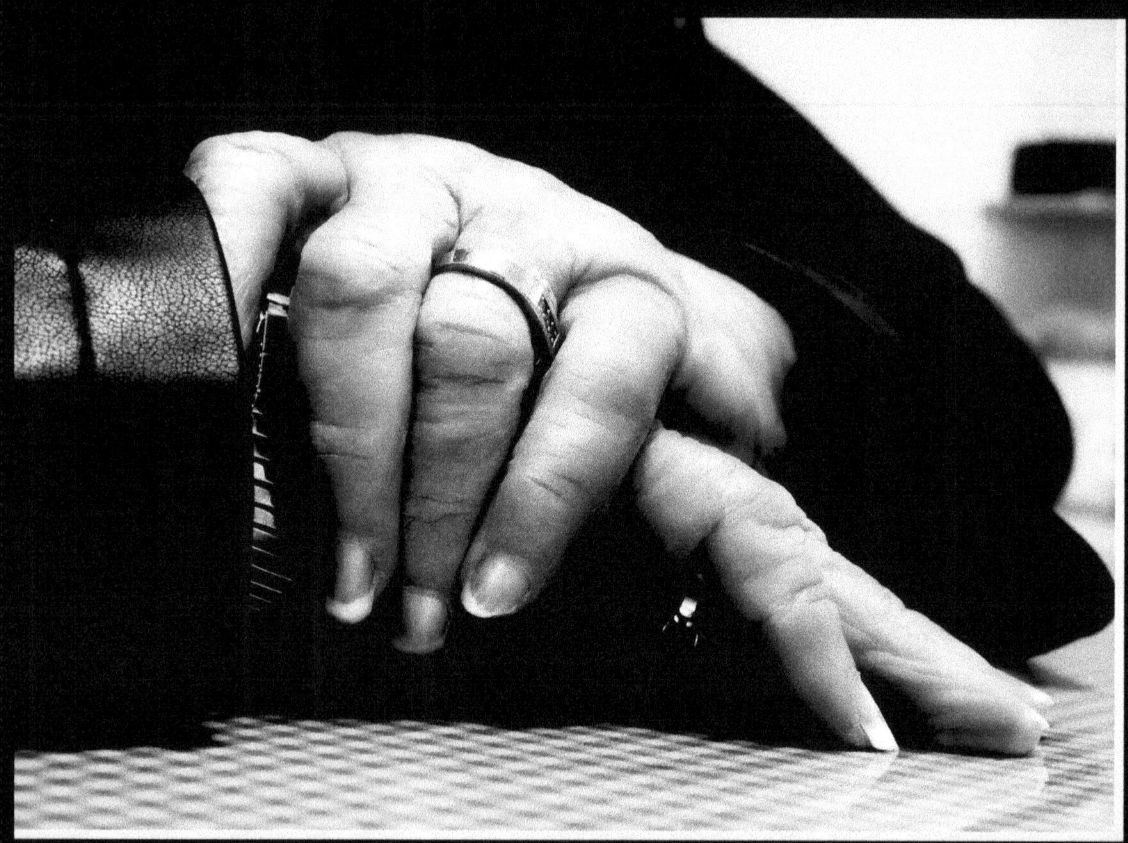

*"I guess in a way,*
*I was learning my father's job for that eventful day."*

My father was a Station Hand on a large sheep and cattle station at Werris Creek, New South Wales. I adored my father and being an only child, I followed him everywhere. I guess in a way, I was learning his job for that eventful day.

One day, my father had an accident on the station and severely injured his back. So severe, he couldn't do his job any longer. Our only home was the house we lived in on the station. We would have to leave. With nowhere to go and little money I stepped up and took on his job – a man's job. I became the bread winner in the family. I was just fourteen years old, small, wiry and full of energy.

My hands were constantly busy. My day began early in the mornings milking about ten cows. Then I'd ride the boundary fence and repaired the timber posts and barbed wire. It was a large station and took half a day to ride the boundary.

The water troughs needed to be filled in droughts. I would chop wood each day for the stove and heating the house. It was very cold in winter, so I chopped a lot of wood.

Once a week I would have to kill and butcher a sheep for the owners of the station. I wasn't very tall, so I would have to get one of the men to hang the sheep up in the tree so I could skin, gut and cut it up.

At times I would also have to slaughter a cow. I would skin and cure the hide, then in my spare time I would plait the skin for stock whips.

I would have to check the horse's hooves regularly if they needed re shoeing.

I was a pretty good with a rifle. Shooting rabbits at night when their numbers increased and shoot foxes for their skins – that was extra money for dad, mum and me.

When sheep needed to go to market, I'd take around 300 head to town with my dogs. Those working dogs did the job of several men if they were trained well. You just had to know how to control them and keep the sheep together.

There were no schools near the station, so Mum taught me some basic education for about 3 years at home when I was very young. I didn't have much interest in what they wanted me to learn with school subjects. Instead, I loved tagging along with my dad while he worked. Anyway, even if I did have any interest, there was no time to learn once I took on dad's job.

*Some children had to step up and step into jobs regardless of their gender.*

## Time is a traveller...Tenterfield, New South Wales...

As soon as I saw the 'Tenterfield' road sign, I began belting out the song; "Time is a traveller, Tenterfield saddler, turn your head, right again jackaroo, think I see kangaroo up ahead..." OK it is an age thing that I can remember the song! But I just had to sing it as loudly as I could to somehow embrace the essence of this country town. This was an iconic Aussie song that became well renowned across the globe and instilled a pride in the country.

Many people became aware of Tenterfield when our internationally acclaimed entertainer, Peter Allen released his touching song 'Tenterfield Saddler' in 1972. It was an emotionally heartfelt account of his early life and a tribute to his grandfather who was a saddler in Tenterfield. The small saddlery store still stands for travellers to visit, and yes his grandfather's name is proudly displayed in the local library as mentioned in the song.

A few years later, Allen released 'I Still Call Australia Home' which has become a rather emotional, heart rendering song, stirring up the sentiments of a deep attachment and pride for our country, our 'home'. Defining and capturing our Australian spirit in modern terms, it has become an unofficial timeless anthem and continues to be sung at major events. The song was also used in several Qantas advertising campaigns during the late 90's and early 2000's. More like a short film extravaganza with a powerful children's choir using our bold mesmerising landscapes as their 'stage' to showcase our country against world icons.

Tenterfield also shared a significant time in Australian history when Sir Henry Parkes, Premier of the Colony of New South Wales delivered his famous Federation Speech in 1889. Calling for the Federation of the six self-governing Australian colonies to later become the foundation of the Commonwealth of Australia. Tenterfield became known as the 'Birthplace of our Nation'.

Stepping back in time a little further, to the mid 1800's, Sir Stuart Donaldson owned a property in the New England area of New South Wales with 18,000 sheep, called Tenterfield Station, named after a region in Scotland. The town also took on the name. The climate of the area was more familiar for our early settlers with cold winters which was also suitable for a majority of our sheep population.

Wandering the town to learn of its history and asking numerous people if they knew anyone who I could talk to with who had a connection to sheep. Tenterfield wasn't as easy as the very small towns but you just have to keep persisting. Someone suggested I try the nursing home.

This is where I met Bob, a joyful, tall gentleman farmer in his late 80's. His family now runs the sheep station just out of town. He felt frustrated that he could no longer physically work on the station and believed he didn't belong in the home at this point in his life. Although it was only due to the physical demands that prevented him working and living on the station any longer. Farming is a lifestyle than merely a job.

*'Looking after 5,000 sheep was a lot of hard work...'*

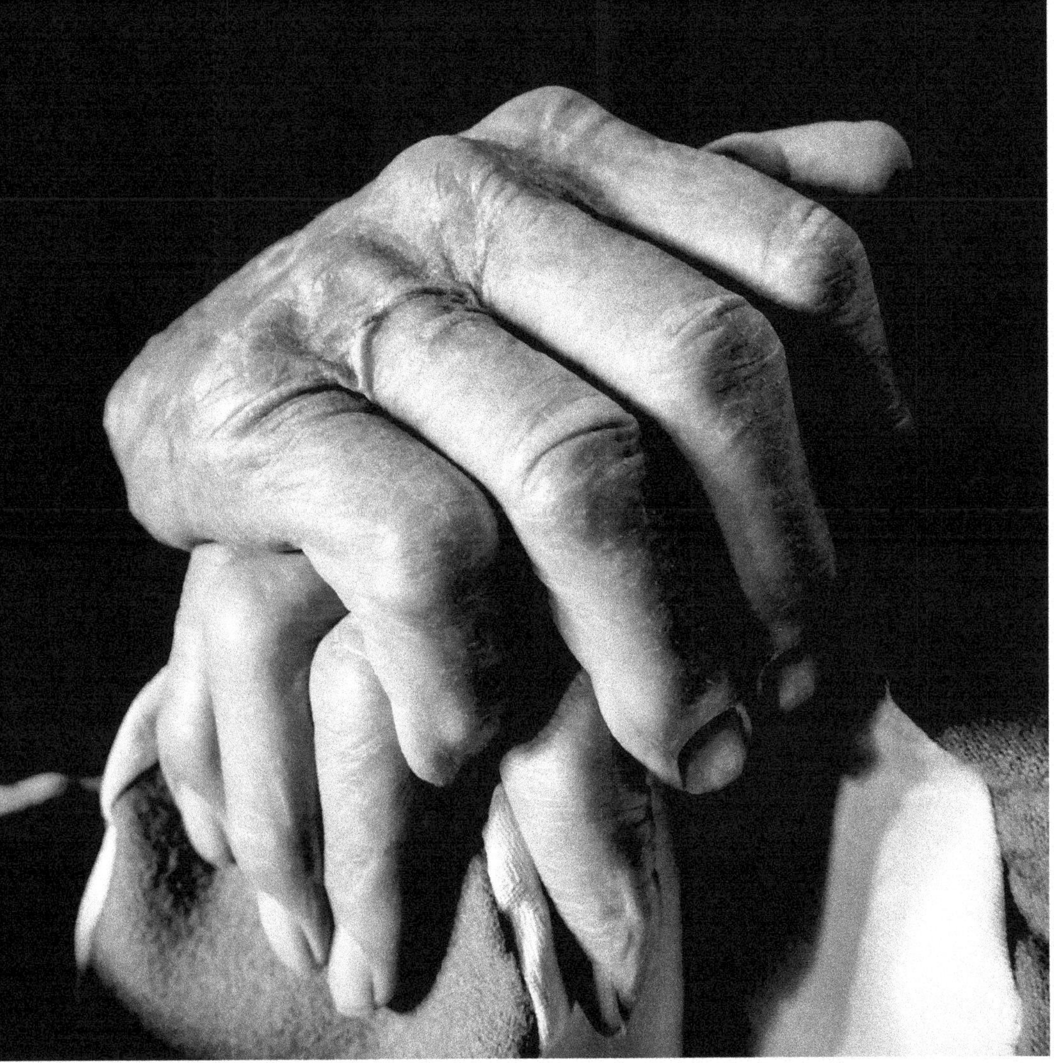

*"Looking after 5,000 sheep was a lot of work on your own."*

I began riding horses by myself around six (years old), before that I used to sit in front of my father in his saddle. You learn to ride by watching and feel. At the same time I began looking after the chooks as my job. As each year passed, I took on more jobs and responsibility on the station. Learning the ways and how a station is run effectively from season to season.

Work on the sheep station was constant. You begin work at sunrise and finish at sunset, seven days a week, year round. Sheep need a lot of attention and maintenance. You are always using your hands in some way and some jobs can be unpleasant, but you just do it.

You would need to check the sheep all the time throughout summer. There is nothing pretty about seeing a sheep that is 'blow ridden'. Blowflies would lay their eggs around the backside of the sheep. You have to clip off the maggots before they ate into the sheep's flesh. It could be a horrible, slow death for an animal. Sometimes you had to help deliver the lambs with your hands when the ewes were having difficulty in delivery.

Looking after 5,000 sheep is a lot of work on your own.

I'd hire 4-5 shearers each shearing season and I'd shear the stragglers.

We'd slaughter cows in winter and sheep in summer for our own meat. The meat needed to be salted and kept cooled because there was no refrigeration back then.

You rode the fence line to constantly maintain the fences, fixing posts and the barbed wire.

We milked the cows twice a day – it was then separated to make cream, cheese and butter.

You chopped all the wood for cooking and heating. There was no electricity in the home back then.

You also needed to look after the working dogs. Feeding them and training them to herd the sheep. Good working dogs did the work of many men rounding up the sheep.

The war broke out and I registered at 17 (years of age), enlisted at 18 (years of age) and fought in Papua New Guinea for four years. When I came home from the war, I went back to work on the station. It is a healthy lifestyle with a lot of hard work, a good life.

*Numerous farms and stations around Australia were instrumental to growing the sheep industry into the prosperity and economical success of our country.*

## An indelible history lesson in Cowra in New South Wales...

Travelling no doubt broadens your mind. All your senses are heightened when you stand on the land, touch the artefacts, view images and listen to people's stories who owns a piece of that history. They create indelible history lessons. That's why I always make a point to visit local museums and chat to a few older locals in each town I visit.

Cowra township itself is a living museum to significant events during the 1940's. So what happened in this little country town? Cowra was home to a Military Training Camp and Prisoner of War Camps during WWII. The museum houses over 4,000 photographic portraits of the soldiers who trained at the camp before they embarked to war destinations across the globe. It also houses images and artefacts from the POW camps which are positioned across the landscape.

It is a sad, yet an important reminder of the horrors of war for all involved and the peace and respect which comes from our worst times. During 1944, around 1,100 Japanese POW's attempted a mass breakout where 231 POW's died and 108 were injured. A good number were killed during the escape by military personnel, some committed suicide while others were killed by their own countrymen. Sadly, many had wanted death, seeing their only way to wipe out the shame for their families and country for being captured. Four Australian soldiers were also killed during the breakout. It was the largest breakout in the Commonwealth's history.

In 1992 Cowra's significant contribution and long standing efforts to peace and international understanding were recognised. The World Peace Bell was awarded signifying in the hope that world peace and world friendship will be realised. The bell weighs in at a hefty 447kgs, cast from melted down medals and coins from member countries of the United Nations.

The town built 12 sprawling acres of beautiful walking Japanese Gardens and a special War Cemetery for the POW's and other Japanese servicemen who died on our soil during this time. Totalling around 520 manicured graves. It is the only Japanese war cemetery outside of Japan.

Cowra is a testament to the people of the past and present for their continued spirit and respect for 'all' who were involved in WWII. At the time of the POW escape, several of the recaptured Japanese prisoners retold their stories of locals feeding them and sometimes giving directions to continue their escape. The trait of giving someone a 'fair go' shone through the town. Many understood the prisoners were soldiers/people just like ours, following orders.

Whilst camping at the local showgrounds, I asked the gentleman in charge if he knew someone which fitted my criteria. He mentioned several people and by chance, a few days later Jeb arrived at the showgrounds to do some much needed maintenance work.

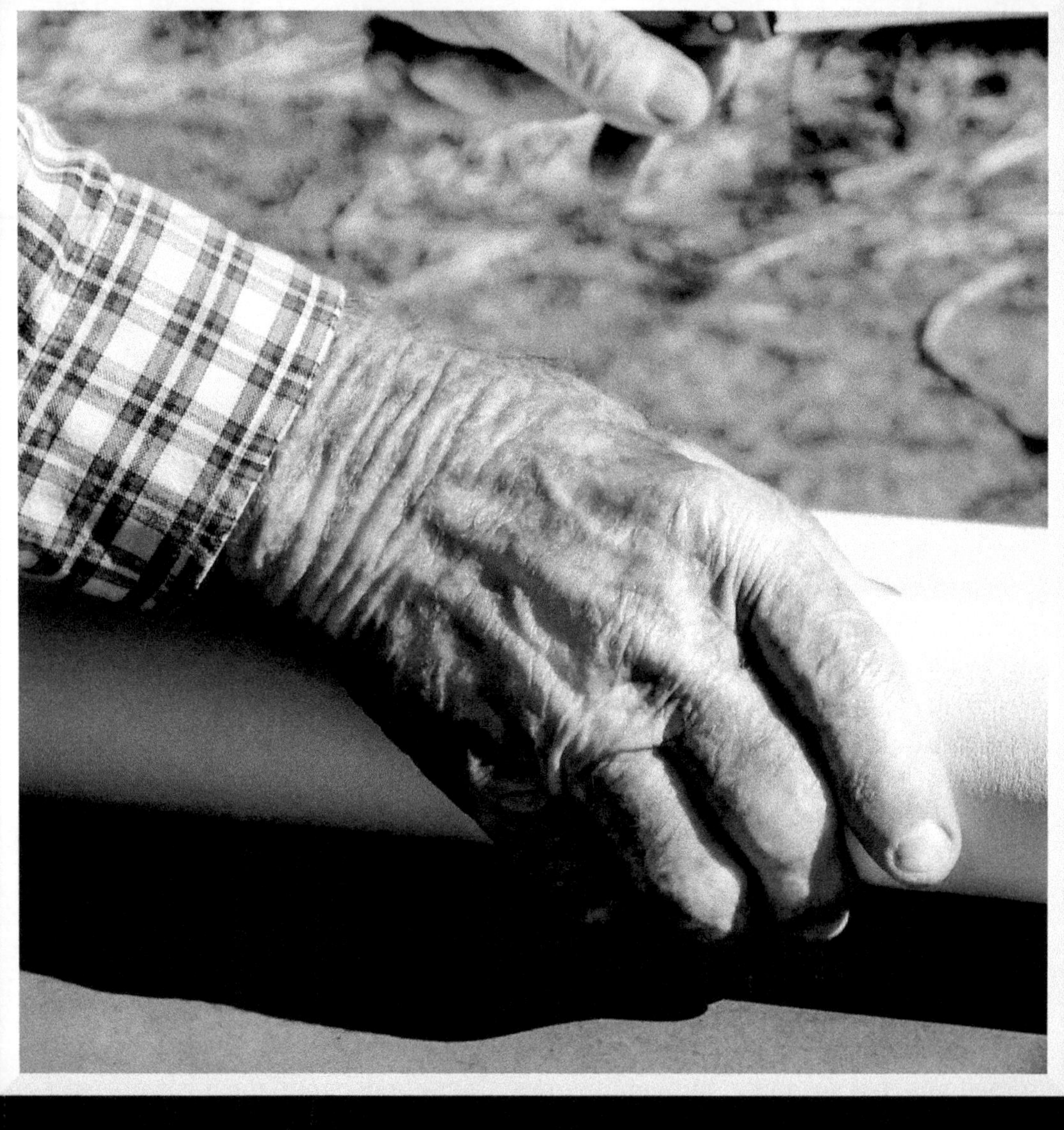

*'Your hands would be drenched in arsenic...'*

*"Your hands would be drenched with arsenic and carbolic disinfectant from the sheep dips."*

I'm a 3rd generation farmer from Irish heritage. I came from a large family, four boys and five girls.

We worked the farm on our own – only employing 2 shearers at shearing time. My wife would muster the sheep on horseback. We worked every day from sun up to sundown.

We cross bred about 1,700 ewes on 1,100 acres. We grew barley and wheat crops for feed grain and to sell.

Everything is done with your hands on a farm. At times, your hands would be drenched with arsenic, carbolic disinfectant and organic phosphate when you are dipping the sheep. You just washed it off with cold water back then. At the time, we didn't know how dangerous it could be on your skin.

Sometimes you have to deliver lambs when the ewes were distressed and the lamb was in breach position. You didn't use gloves, you have to roll the lamb inside of the ewe and pull the lamb out.

When you weren't looking after the sheep, you were planting the crops, repairing fences, building, repairing the house and sheds and pruning the fruit trees.

We killed our own lambs and salted the meat so it would keep. We didn't have refrigerators back then.

You always helped neighbours with different jobs. That's the way of life, farming has a strong sense of community.

These are farmer's hands – hunter's hands - butcher's hands. Your hands just toughened up over the years with all the work, but they didn't wear out. (chuckling)

*Many Australians were European descendants who came from cold climates. The harsh sun and dry conditions weren't ideal for their naturally pale skin colouring. Their exposed hands browned and hardened, their skin thickened over the years.*

# Harnessing our most precious commodity

Australia is the most arid habitable continent on the planet. The quest for fresh water supplies to grow crops and feed livestock was a constant obstacle for expanding the country. Its lack created heartbreaking droughts, loss of life and unproductive soils to grow our nation's food and sustain our growing population.

The remarkable feat of engineering and labour intensive Snowy Mountain Scheme was an absolute must story to include. Its execution was a complex marvel on a world stage. It played a significant role to harness and manage Australia's most precious commodity, water. The volumes of water flowing from the Snowy Mountains' range provided hydroelectric power and water irrigation security to the south east region of our country.

The scheme was constructed over a staggering 5,000 square kilometres in alpine wilderness with only 2% being visible from above ground. Consisting of 225 kilometres of trans-mountain tunnels, pipelines and aqueducts, sixteen dams, seven power stations and two pumping stations. Generating over 65% of renewable energy to Victoria and New South Wales. This scheme was an astounding achievement for its time and still highly praised by today's standards.

Construction began in 1949 and took 25 years to construct. Over 100,000 people were employed, where 70% were immigrant workers, representing 30 countries. The immigrants were seeking a new life after the chaos of WWII and many provided the much needed engineering skills and expertise which our country lacked at the time.

A high proportion of work was carried out by hand in the early years. Many sets of hands working in freezing winter conditions. Viewing images of the construction with men hanging from mere ropes over vertical, wet and slippery mountains was a work safety nightmare by today's standards.

Desperately wanting to hear stories from earlier workers, I tried many avenues without success. The reason being; in the past journalists, film makers and production companies had twisted and highly dramatized their stories. Apparently, there were a few conflicts between nationality's resentments towards their former enemies so soon after the war. However, I was told by a few people, it was nowhere near the scale it had been depicted.

Supposedly, one senior engineer pulled a group together saying, 'We are all new Australians. This is a title which is not to be abused. The nonsense of Europe has no place here.' Apparently, the issues quickly died down with their driving focus on this massive project and opportunity for a new life in a new country was put into perspective. I totally understood and respected their reluctance to tell me their stories.

***People came together for something larger than themselves, our future's growth and survival.***

# A nation's legend lives in our High Country

The High Country holds a rich and fascinating history where stories and legends were born, and where wild brumbies roam free.

Australia's 'High Country' sits in the Alpine region of NSW & Victoria with a spectacular array of seasonal landscapes. Each year, brilliant white snow begins to melt on misty mountain ranges, marking the end of the winter playground season. The mountains spring to life with tiny coloured alpine flowers blanketing lush green landscapes. Water gushes down the mountains feeding the trout filled streams. Following the folds down through the pine and eucalypt forested valleys, this water has a purpose. It eventually settles for a while, giving birth to the mighty Murray River. This valuable water supply then begins to flow through the land dispersing its life force to farm lands 100's of kilometres away.

European settlers arrived in the area in the early 1800's, mainly for grazing cattle. The mountain landscape is dotted with historic, rustic huts where the cattlemen lived during the changing seasons of the year. These mountain cattlemen would move their livestock up into the High Country for summer grazing and muster them back home through the hills, creeks and wooded lands before the snow fell each year.

While hiking through this picturesque alpine countryside, if you stop and listen hard enough, you'll hear the echoes of bygone days. Stock whips cracking to the thunderous sounds of horse hooves racing through the hills. Stockmen retelling local tales around the pitch of hissing camp fires. One of those tales was of a legendary ride that inspired a poet and captured the heart of a nation.

The High Country was the setting for one of Australia's most famous bush poems, 'The Man from Snowy River'. AB 'Banjo' Patterson penned this poem not long after he met with the local Jack Riley who supposedly rode down a nail biting, sheer hill in hot pursuit of a breakaway colt and a mob of strong-willed wild brumbies. The poem immortalised the tale and became an influential part of Australia's identity world-wide with the release of a film of the same name.

The district holds many intriguing stories. Tales of notorious bushranger's exploits who possessed abundant survival skills to live and hide in the bush from authorities. Ruthless, lawless bushrangers such as Ned Kelly and his gang, 'Mad Dog' Morgan and Harry Power strangely became folk heroes to many Australians. Surely this attitude of admiration streamed from our convict's symbol of rebellion against the authorities. These glorified tales remain a rich part of our heritage.

***Inspiring tales that moulded our identity.***

## Recreating a nation's tale in Corryong in Victoria...

Nestled in the foothills of the magnificent High Country lies the town of Corryong. A fortunate time to arrive, a week before the exciting annual 'Man from Snowy River Bush Festival'. This is an amazing opportunity to 'step into' Banjo Patterson's iconic poem that moved a nation. I grew up reciting this poem while visualising the epic scenes unfold as told throughout the story.

The legend and inspiration of the ride through the hills lives on over the festival's four days. Australia's finest horsemen and horsewomen gather each year to be crowned the title 'The Man (and Woman) from Snowy River' in a series of events and challenges, including the thrilling Brumby Catch. It also includes a host of other events including whip cracking, working cattle dogs, rodeo rides, bush poetry, a bullock team and many more events.

The highlight for me was watching Banjo Patterson's poem come to life in a superb re-enactment at sunrise in the nearby rolling hills. Coinciding with an expressive narrative from a gentleman slowly riding a white horse before us with all the action of the story line unfolding in the background. For me, it was a chilling moment, witnessing some of the best riders in the land. The whole scene infused visions of the romanticised cattleman's life of the High Country.

Wanting to embrace and be part of this classic celebration in some way, donning a bush hat I nervously recited an original bush poem on stage at the festival's Poet's Corner. It was a rather poor, wooden performance on my part. However the opportunity to step into this piece of our heritage was too good an opportunity to miss. Even if it was for a few fleeting minutes, I had an illusion of being part of the High Country rather than being a mere observer. I have to say there are some very serious poets and narrators who walk onto that stage.

It was an opportune and hectic time when pride for the bygone days was heightened. Many of the locals had come to town for the festival, so it was relatively easy to ask around to be able to meet someone and hear their stories.

One lady's name came up a few times. Locating her son, I explained my purpose and asked if he could be present when I spoke to his mother. He laughed and said, 'she will tell you within five minutes if she doesn't like you, she doesn't need me there'. Hmm, obviously I would be meeting a very strong willed lady. Contacting Joan to arrange a time to meet, she told me it had later in the week as she was heavily involved in the festival. I saw Joan riding her beloved horse at the re-enactment and again in the street parade. This lady was in her eighties with long brilliant red plaited hair and still horse riding! I was very intrigued to hear her story.

Another name which came up a few times was Len's. He called himself a Bushman, a Jack of all Trades. We sat on his porch listening to the wide variety of jobs he tackled over his lifetime. Len was an incredibly positive person who loved his life and proud of all the types of work he tackled in his life. He even showed me his saddle making tools, which he still dabbles in repairs today.

Visiting Corryong's museum, a gentleman told me of a husband and wife who were generational farmers, Boy and Marlene. Boy's grandparent's settled in the area as farmers in the late 1800's. It was fascinating to hear both a male and female's roles on a farm. Boy called it a dairy farm, yet they also carried large numbers of sheep. They were quite self-sufficient living on the farm, raising or making almost everything they ate and wore.

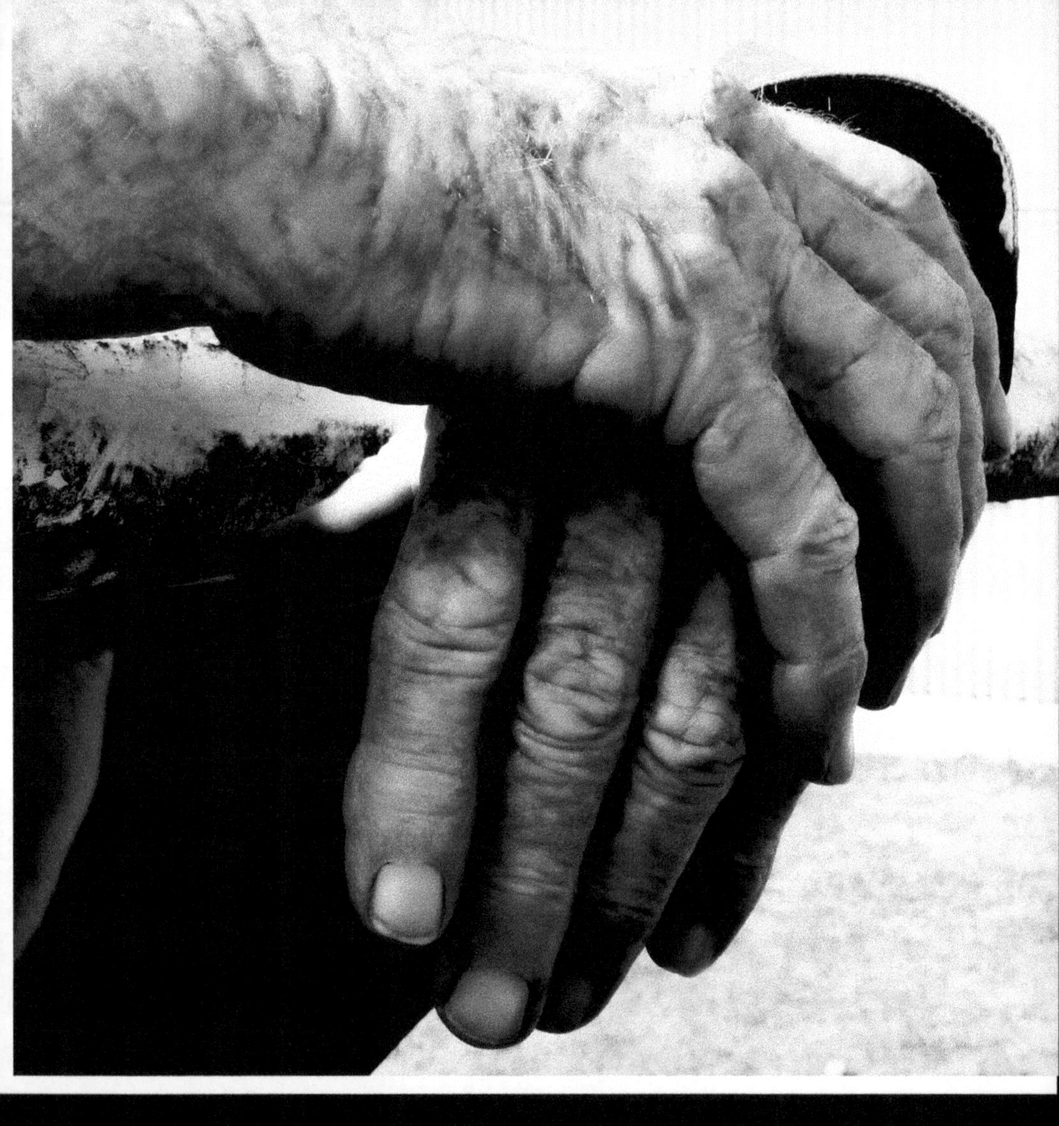

*'I bought this farm and kept it going through many hardships...'*

*"I bought this farm and I kept it going through many hardships."*

Mum and Dad had a dairy farm, Dad was also a Drover.

I was always a bit of a spirited tomboy climbing fences. I'd ride my horse 10 miles to school each day across the rivers and backwater in these hills. I was always a good horse rider, I even became a jockey for a while when I was younger.

There was always a lot of jobs to do. Milking the cows, hand feeding the poddy calves. I'd deliver calves, foals and lambs. I'd pump water, skin sheep, cut snakes and drove tractors. I looked after the vegetable beds, trees, chickens. I love my birds, I now have an aviary with a large variety of birds.

I was always good with a rifle and I'm still a good aim. I raised, bred and sold cattle for years, I had around 200 Hereford cattle on this farm at any one time.

I trained local racehorses and trained working dogs, did a lot of men's work. I wasn't your typical female, and didn't have much interest in cooking or baking like other women, I only cooked what was necessary. I liked to be physically active around the farm every day.

I married twice and nursed both husbands for years when they became ill, until they passed away. I'd worked hard all my life, saving enough to eventually buy Mum and Dad's farm, I love this place. I bought up two children for long periods by myself and worked hard all my life.

I've kept this farm going through many hardships over the years. Cared for it and made it what it is today. I still look after the farm today, although I don't have as many cattle as I used to. I still ride my horses around the farm and in local events, they are my love, so are my dogs.

*You have to be tough and speak your mind in life to survive. That's how I got by.*
*Some women are naturally strong and become stronger out of necessity.*
*There are many legendary stories of people from this Snow Mountain region*
*and Joan is one of those people.*

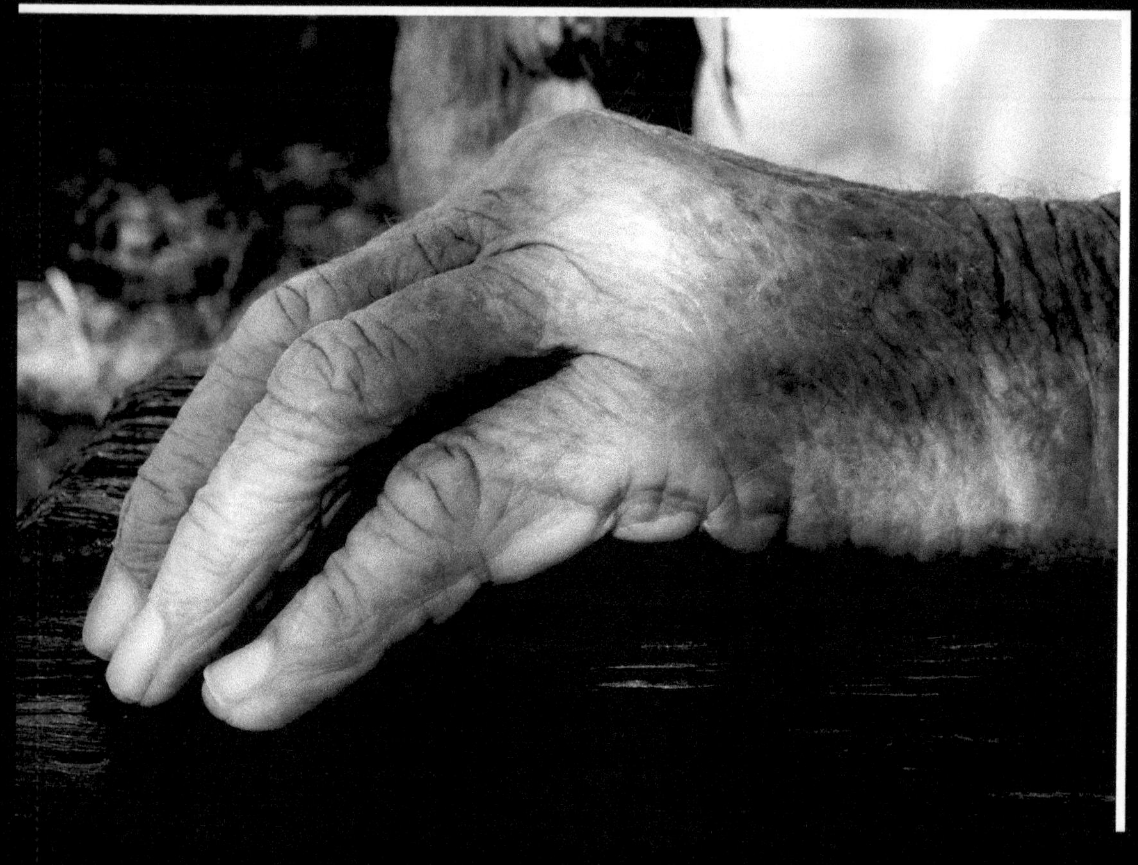

*'Farming is a way of life,
you don't think of it as a job,
but it's a lot of hard work...'*

*"Farming is a way of life,
you don't think of it as a job, but it's constant hard work."*

I'm from a farming family, I grew up on a farm. My grandparents settled around here in 1896 and built a farm.

Farming is a way of life, you don't think of it as a job, but its constant hard work. You work to a routine that comes from years of experience. Work begins around 7.30am until sundown. We didn't have electricity for twelve years. We used kerosene lamps for light and a wood fired stove for cooking and heating the house in winter. You have to chop a lot of wood for winter.

You know what needs to be done each day and then there are the unexpected things that turn up. There's always time, because you live and work on the farm, you make the time.

There are a lot of different things to do, so you have to know how to do everything. It was just my wife and myself working the farm in the beginning.

It's a dairy farm with 150 cows and calves and about 800-3,000 sheep, depending on the year.

We had pigs, chooks and five to six Kelpie working dogs. You always have a cat to catch the mice around the farm.

You have to know about all the animals. What to do when the animals are sick, if the calves are getting enough milk and helping the animals give birth if there are any complications. Shearing the sheep, sheep dips. Protecting to chooks from foxes.

You have a rifle and a shotgun for snakes that come too close to the house or to shoot foxes and rabbits. Sometimes you have to put an animal down if they are too sick or badly injured. Life and death is part of farming.

It wasn't just the farm animals that needed looking after. You grew your own vegetables and had plenty of fruit trees that needed pruning. You'd milk the cows. You kill sheep and cows for their meat.

There was a lot of different work that need to be done each day.

*We owe much to our early farmers who carved out the
land for grazing and cropping despite the challenges for
fresh water in the most arid country in the world.
With hard work and ingenuity from many,
Australia became a premier food producing country for
over 100 years from the 1840's to the 1950's.*

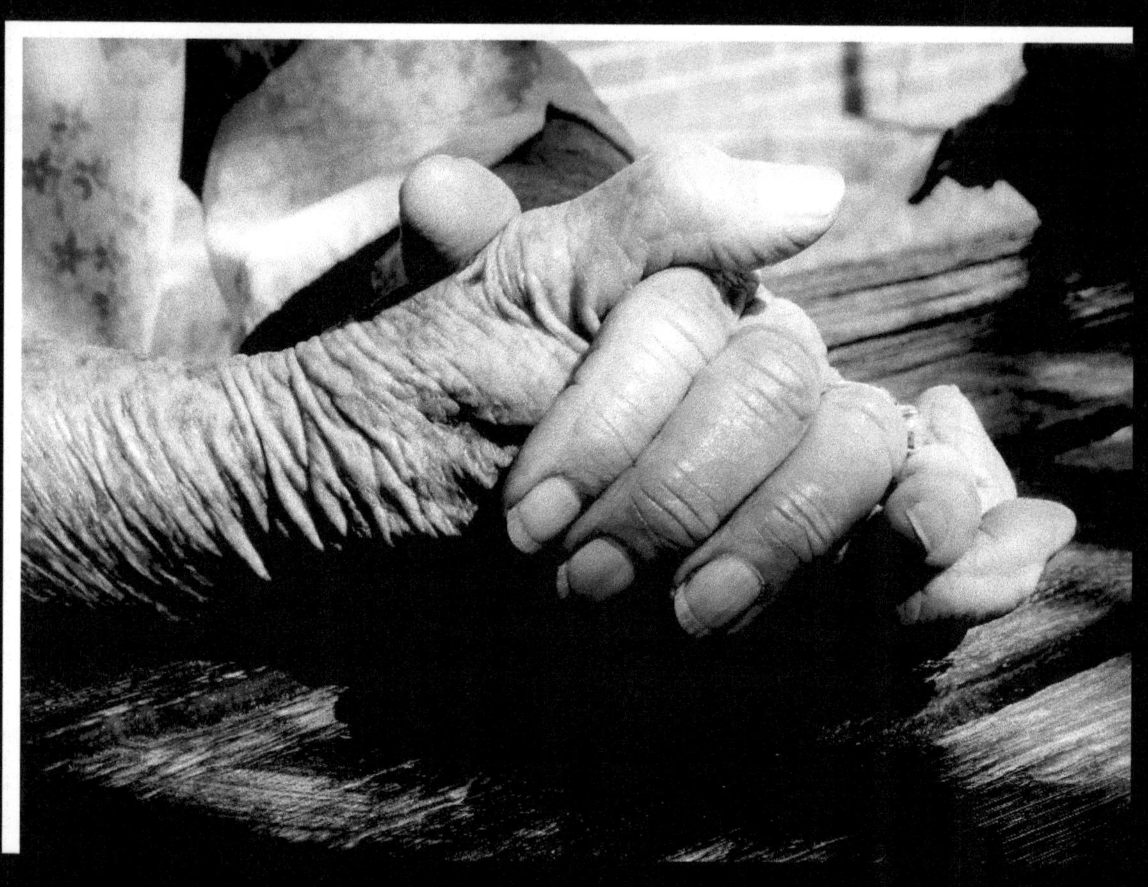

*'Your hands were always busy,
there were many things to do each day...'*

*"Your hands were always busy.*
*There were many things to do every day."*

We had no electricity on the farm for the first twelve years. We used wood for heating and kerosene lamps for light. There certainly were no kitchen gadgets, all food was prepared by hand.

Once a month we would ride to town to buy sacks of flour, sugar and tea.

I knitted clothing for the family from our sheep's fleece and alpaca wool. Combing and spinning the wool would take five hours to make a skene.

Your hands were always busy. There were many things to do every day from sunrise to sunset.

I'd wash the clothes using a washing board in a tub of water. It was cold work in winter, the water was not heated and dirty work clothes needed more time to scrub clean. I used a flat iron that was heated over the wood fired stove.

We had a large vegetable garden and fruit trees. Four apple trees, a pear tree, plumb tree and a peach tree. We ate the fruit when it was ripe and I would bottle the rest so we could eat fruit throughout the year. We also had chickens which laid many eggs each week. We had milk from the cows and made our own butter and cheese. We always had plenty of food and it was a healthy diet and we had a good variety of food.

We'd slaughter lambs throughout the year and occasionally a cow for our meat. It all had to be salted and kept cool and moist using hessian bags so it would keep and not go off, because we had no refrigerator.

The house had to be swept each day from the dirt that would blow in or walked in. You had to keep up with the dusting too.

Much later in life we gradually bought a few kitchen gadgets and a radio when we finally got electricity to the farm. It made life a little easier and gave us more time for other things.

When I look back at those early years on the farm, it was tough work, but I liked the simpler life in some ways.

Farmer's wives are the unsung heroes. Their roles were many.

*They maintained the household, prepare meals for their husband and workers and they often rolled their sleeves up and helped their husbands with the heavier farm work. Farmers usually ate robust, high calorie foods in large portions. Salted meats, bacon, eggs, cream, butter, bread. Yet, their long periods of physical manual labour easily burnt the calories. The food was wholesome and natural, with no added chemicals or preservatives (aside from salt).*

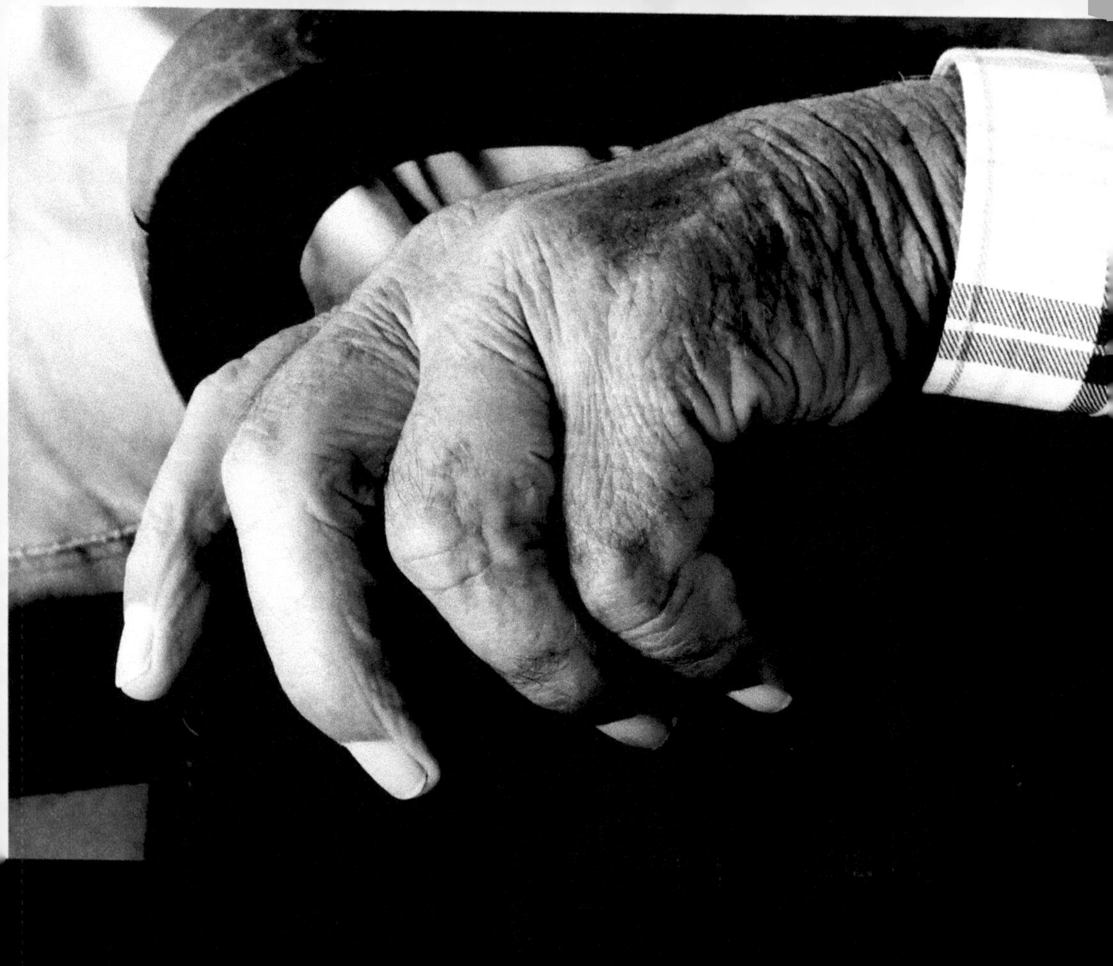

*'You had to put your hand to any job that's going.'*

*"You had to put your hand to any job that's going."*

I was a Bushman, a Jack of all Trades. You had to be adaptable to put your hand to any job that's going and you need to have a lot of common sense.

I began working in my early teens and worked side by side with men, older men. I grew up quick. There was no consideration for your age, you had to do a man's job and keep up with them. I would listen to the stories of the WWI Diggers, Bushmen, farmers and gold miners. I learnt a lot about work and life from those stories.

During shearing season, I could sheer about 120 sheep in a day, which wasn't bad at all. We used manual shears, not those electric clippers. You had to be quick and safe. Clipping the wool so close to the skin you could nick their skin. If you did, a boy in the shed would put a dob of tar on it to stop the bleeding.

Working on the sheep farms, you have to push sheep into the sheep dips made up of arsenic and sulphur, it would splash on your hands and clothing all day long. You didn't realise how dangerous those chemicals were back then, but we survived.

I'd worked with a blacksmith for a while and learnt the trade which came in handy with other jobs.

I split a lot of fence posts for dairy farms. I'd use a wide broad axe, seven foot long. Did a lot of wood chopping too.

Another thing I learned was to repair saddles. It was quite a craft to learn and I did it well. I still have all my tools and dabble with some repairs now.

It was an active life and I loved using my hands, feeling life, everything was alive. I really liked learning new things, it stimulated the head too.

I loved the variety of work and was always proud to do a good job with anything I did.

*Early Australian Bushmen were idealised by their pioneering spirit, resourcefulness and resilience. Out of sheer necessity, the need to survive in the remote areas of the bush you had to know how to do a lot of different jobs. It was a transient, tough and sometimes a tragic life in the early years.*

# A Tropical Paradise – North Queensland

'Beautiful one day, perfect the next' was the highly successful tourism slogan encouraging tourists to visit Queensland's outstanding tropical coastline.

Tropical Queensland is a glamorous paradise where you escape the weary winters for sunshine and warmth. A place to 'take it easy' as you casually explore World Heritage Listed tropical rainforests or kick back on one of the many idyllic islands which seemingly float in the azure blue waters over the world's largest coral reef system, the renown Great Barrier Reef. Sampling the sweet exotic fruits which grow year round in the rich basalt soils. Ahh Tropical Queensland is nature's colourful playground to dream of an exotic tranquil existence for the rest of your life.

I'd spent many idyllic holidays exploring this 'perfect' paradise throughout my life. Yet, this trip had a different purpose, uncovering its history of people who developed the various industries which made this area of Australia successful.

I began exploring how the sugarcane industry began and how pivotal it may have been in Australia's prosperity. While researching this thriving industry, its history as well as seeking out its pioneering people, I remembered that tourism slogan and thought, how far removed was the reality of the early dark side in the expansion of this glorious paradise.

Early Australia was creating new industries across the continent at a rapid rate. John Mackay was reportedly the first European to visit Tropical Queensland. Mackay led an expedition in 1860 to find more potential pastoral land to continue building the foundation of modern Australia. Just one year later, the first settlement was established on the coastline in Bowen to develop sugarcane farming. The sugarcane had to be crushed within 15 hours of being cut to be able to extract the moist sugar juice. Hundreds of sugar mills were built as the sugarcane farming districts grew north along the coast to Mossman. The mills operated 24hours a day for the six months of harvest season.

Sugarcane is now Queensland's largest agricultural crop, producing around 95% of Australian sugar. A staggering 35million tonnes is grown on over 4,000 farms along Queensland's northern coastline.

In the past, convicts took up most of the grisly, back-breaking work in developing cities, towns, industries, pastoral and agricultural lands. However, after 80 years, convict transportation was coming to an end around the time Tropical Queensland was being developed. Vast tracks of virgin land had to be cleared with hard physical labour to create sugarcane farms and the free convict labour was no longer available.

There were great concerns from authorities if European workers could endure working in the searing heat and high humidity in North Queensland. So, an estimated 62,000 Pacific Islanders and Northern Australia's Indigenous people were 'recruited' to clear the land and build the sugarcane industry. Some came willingly while others were 'kidnapped' by coercion or trickery with the practice of 'Blackbirding'. The workers were termed 'indentured labourers' as the workers signed 'contracts'. A rather shaky technically as most could not read nor write.

This practice continued for forty years until 1901 with the introduction of the Federation's White Australia Policy. The vast majority of Pacific Islanders were abruptly deported in line with the policy, yet there was more work in the industry to be executed.

Around this time, the government began recruiting Italian people to replace the labour force on the sugarcane farms. Many current sugarcane growers in this area are descendants of the early Italian cane cutters who worked tirelessly in the extreme heat from sunrise to sunset, saving everything they earnt to buy farms of their own.

The thick foliage of the cane stalks created shade and homes for rats, snakes and a host of animals and insects. In the early years, quite a number of men died from Weil's disease which was carried by rat's urine infecting any cuts men had on their body. In 1936 a court action declared all sugarcane had to be burnt prior to cutting in the Ingham district to kill the disease. Burning the cane fields prior to cutting became a practice with all sugarcane farms until the introduction of machinery.

I tried to locate descendants of the 'Blackbirders' who remained in Australia to perhaps hear their passed down stories of their ancestors. Unfortunately, the conversations were mainly general information rather than individual stories to be included in this book.

***A not so perfect paradise, created a prosperous future.***

## Fond childhood memories in Mackay in Queensland...

Photographing the bright green sugarcane stalks sway in the tropical breeze bought back fond childhood memories. Our family holidayed each year along the east coast of Australia during harvest season. Occasionally, burnt sugarcane stalks would fall from the trucks and cane trains as they hauled immense tonnes of cane to the sugar mills. We'd eagerly pick up the fallen stalks from the roadside where our father would then cut and split the stalks into small pieces. For the rest of the day, we sucked on the sweet juice from its fibrous centre.

To this day, I can vividly recall watching the dramatic scenes of cane fields burning vigorously. Loud cracking sounds echoed as we watched enormous flames and black smoke filling the blue skies.

On this journey, it was a bit of a mistake to travel through northern Queensland in summer. The humidity was oppressive. I was living in a constant pool of sweat day and night and my tiny 12 centimetre fan was broken. My first night in Mackay was incredibly unbearable, there was no hope of sleeping in my claustrophobic van. So I worked on my computer during the night to fill in time. Around 3am I googled the temperate which was only 38 degrees, yet the humidity was a ghastly 98%. How on earth did the early settlers adjust to living in this extreme weather, working in the fields from sunrise to sunset in their heavy woven clothing and trying to sleep during the nights without cooling devices?

They adapted and ingeniously began building their homes off the ground on tall stumps to cool and ventilate under the floorboards. A lightweight timber construction with wide covered verandas wrapped the home providing shelter from the heat and rains, creating a semi inside/outside living area. It was an open home having a friendly and relaxed attraction, just like the people of the area. This unique style of home became widely known as the 'Queenslander' and is strongly associated with our cultural heritage.

A large percentage of the farms are individually owned, so I knew it was not going to too difficult to find someone to speak with. I began asking in the local country pubs in towns around Mackay. A few phone calls later I had arranged a time to meet with a gentleman who bought a small parcel of land and created his own sugarcane farm.

I met with Monty who was in his late eighties, along with his two daughters at a local community centre the following day.

Monty was a strong, sturdy body of a man with large working hands roughened by the decades of work and extreme weather. It was people like Monty who grew the industry into the success it is today. Starting out with a small block of virgin land and painstakingly clearing the rocks, trees and scrub to create a blank canvas to plant a sugarcane crop.

*'You buy a piece of land,*
*that will one day be a farm...'*

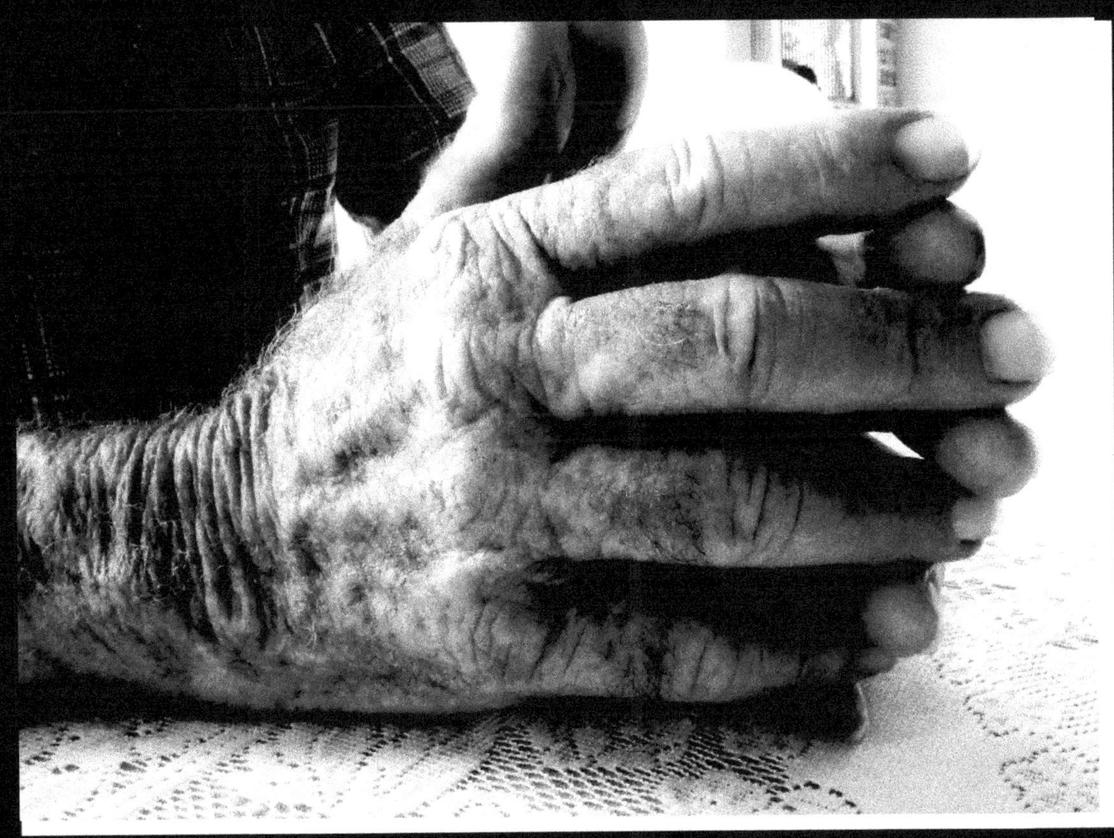

*"You buy a fifteen acre piece of land that will one day be a farm."*

Clearing land is back breaking work. You begin removing all the boulders and rocks, then the trees and scrub. The strain of lifting all the heavy rocks gave me a hernia. But that's just what you had to do.

Then you buy some green cane stalks and cut the cane in one foot pieces in length. Your horse drags two sticks making a drill line, the cane is placed in the furrow and the horses go back and cover them with soil. After that, you wait for the rain and the next summer to cut the cane.

The horses got large sores on their necks from the friction of the yoke in the heat and humidity. We used to pour urine over the sores to help them heal.

In the early years we cut the cane green. Snakes, rats and other vermin lived in the thick foliage of the plants. Men were dying. They soon found that the rat's urine in the cane harvest infected their cuts. They called it Weil's disease. So we began burning the outer foliage before cutting which cleared the vermin and the disease, it also made it easier to cut the cane.

Sometimes the fires would get out of control and destroy the crop. You raced to help the other farmers when the fires grew too large and fierce. We dampened the fires with wet hessian bags and tree branches.

Two days after burning you were ready to cut the cane. We worked from the first light of the day until there was no more light left in the sky. You could cut about 1 acre a day, 10 tonnes of sticky sugarcane.

Swinging an 18 inch curved blade with a wooden handle over your shoulder you cut the cane close to the ground. So hard was your grip that your fingers would leave impressions in the timber over time. You changed your handle each season or two and filed it to fit your hand. The blade would need to be sharpened each day and lasted for about two seasons, if you didn't hit any stray rocks and break it. There were some serious accidents of men cutting their legs or feet.

It was dirty work, the cane was black from the fires. Sugar began sweating from the cane and that attracted bees. Our hands would be stung all the time, but you kept working. Your hands sweat and large blisters form on your palms and fingers, you kept working. Most men would pour urine on their hands to harden the blistered, calloused skin. Others used thick grease at the end of the day to ease the pain.

When all the cane was cut, it was railed it to the sugar mills. You have a little time to rest before planting for the next season. You turned the soil over and over using a hoe drawn by a horse. Then you plant the cut cane and wait for summer to begin the work all over again.

*Successful industries were created by many individual's small successes and their hard work over many decades.*

## Finding the Italian connection in Ingham, Queensland...

Continuing along the coast, numerous people told me of the strong Italian community of sugarcane farmers around Ingham, which lies 100km north of Townsville.

In the 1850's, Outback Queensland already had a small number of Italian settlers working in various industries. Around 1901 a significant number of Italian immigrants began increasing, with a dramatic rise in the 1920's when the Pacific Islander workers were deported with the introduction of the White Australia Policy came into force. About 45% of the sugarcane farms around Ingham, were owned by Italian settlers.

Our early Italian settlers saw opportunities and shaped North Queensland's sugarcane industry through determination and sheer hard work for a better life. Most began working as cane cutters, saving their money to buy a piece of land and create their own cane farm. They saw land ownership was their security for the future.

At the start of WWII, the government built internment camps for people who were classed as 'enemy aliens', people who were nationals of countries at war with Australia. Thousands of men and some women and children were interned in these camps for up to four years. Most were ordinary people who came to Australia to create a life and who meant no harm to our country. However the camps were deemed necessary in the name of national security for the time.

For the Italian sugarcane community, these were tough times. Families were absent of fathers, husbands and brothers for the duration of the war. Male cane cutters and farm workers were in short supply. Women and children had to carry the weight of men's roles of cutting and planting the cane and keep the farms running for several years on their own.

Being a small tight knit community, it was relatively easy to find several Italian farmers who came to Australia in the 1940's. I'd visited a small museum in the district and learnt of a lady named Elsa who now was in her eighties, was a young teenager of Italian parents during WWII. She was still cutting cane on the farm in her seventies and continues to live on the farm tending her garden.

One particular gentleman I met named Peter, came to Australia as a young man and described his trials and struggles to learn English, to communicate and meet young women. He said people were scared of him and other Italians in the early years as they were 'different'. Many Italian workers needed to develop a 'thick skin' with name calling from people's own ignorance at the time.

What I wasn't expecting to find, was a high spirited proud Irish gentleman named Charlie. It had been a dramatic climate shock for this red haired gentleman. He hand cut untold tonnes of cane for sixteen seasons around Ingham to Mossman in Far North Queensland. His feisty spirit is still evident by the way he held his hands – in a fist.

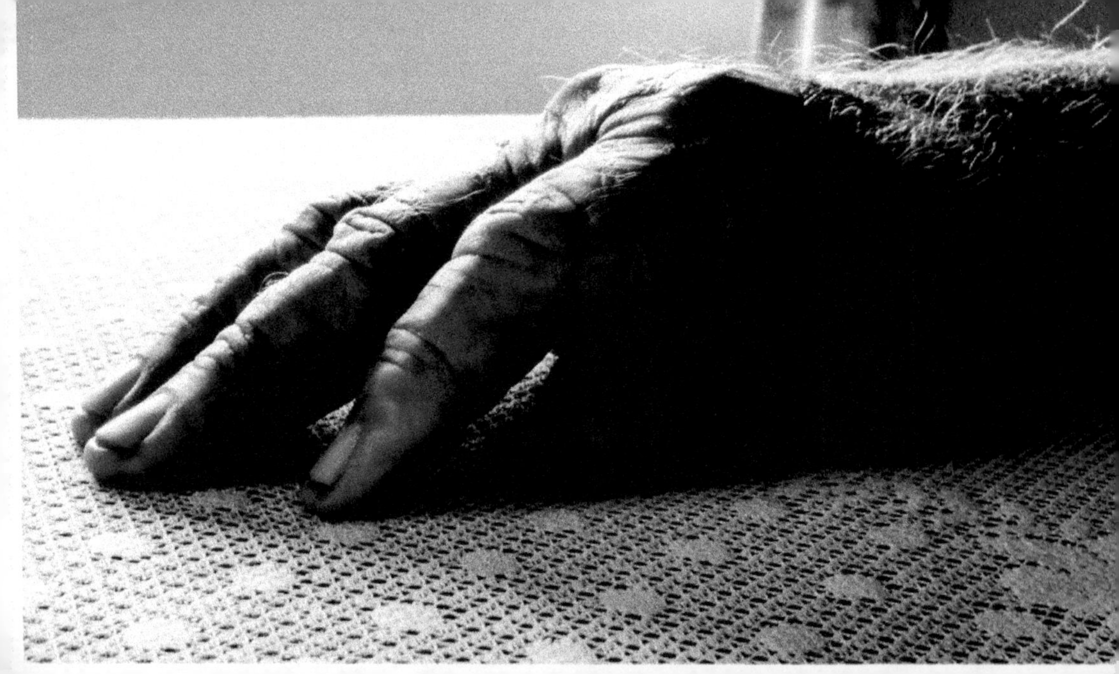

*"We had to keep the farm going somehow,
until our father and brothers were released from the camps."*

I was a baby when we arrived in Australia from Italy. My father bought some farm land up here and soon began planting cane, sugarcane. We also grew our own vegetables and beans. There was a lot to do each day. You had to make do with what you had, although we always had plenty to eat.

With four children in the family, we all had jobs to do. Our mother taught us to cook, pick beans, sew and wash clothing in an old Kerosene tin at an early age.

I went to school by horse and learned English. During harvest I would cut the tops off the cane and mix it with molasses to feed our six horses. I began cutting the cane when I was about 5 years old, I didn't wear any shoes or gloves. I used one of the big cane knives the men used. I put traps out in the fields to catch the rats that lived in the green cane. You didn't want them in your home either. The whole family cut the cane in the early years.

A few years later, the farm was bigger and we had gangs to cut the cane. I would wake up early and cook the men's breakfast and take it into the paddocks before school. Scrambled eggs, bread, cheese and jam, wrapped in hessian bags. They had already been working for a few hours, before the sun rose.

I was a teenager when WWII broke out. My father and two brothers were interned in camps for the duration of the war. So were the other Italian cane farmers and cane cutters. We had to keep the farm going somehow or we'd lose it. There were no men we could employ, so my mother, sister and I cut, planted and burnt the cane. Hauled the bundles of cane into the train carriages and sent them to the sugar mills. We did this for four years until our father and brothers were released from the camp after the war ended. It was very hard work, but we saved the farm and our family was back together again.

I was still working, planting cane in my 70's (years). I never went to a doctor in my life (giggling). I never thought about being sick and I don't think I had time to see a doctor.

*For some families, strength was found with overcoming obstacles.*

*'If you cut 10 tonnes of cane a day,
you would have to throw that 10 tonnes into the carriages.'*

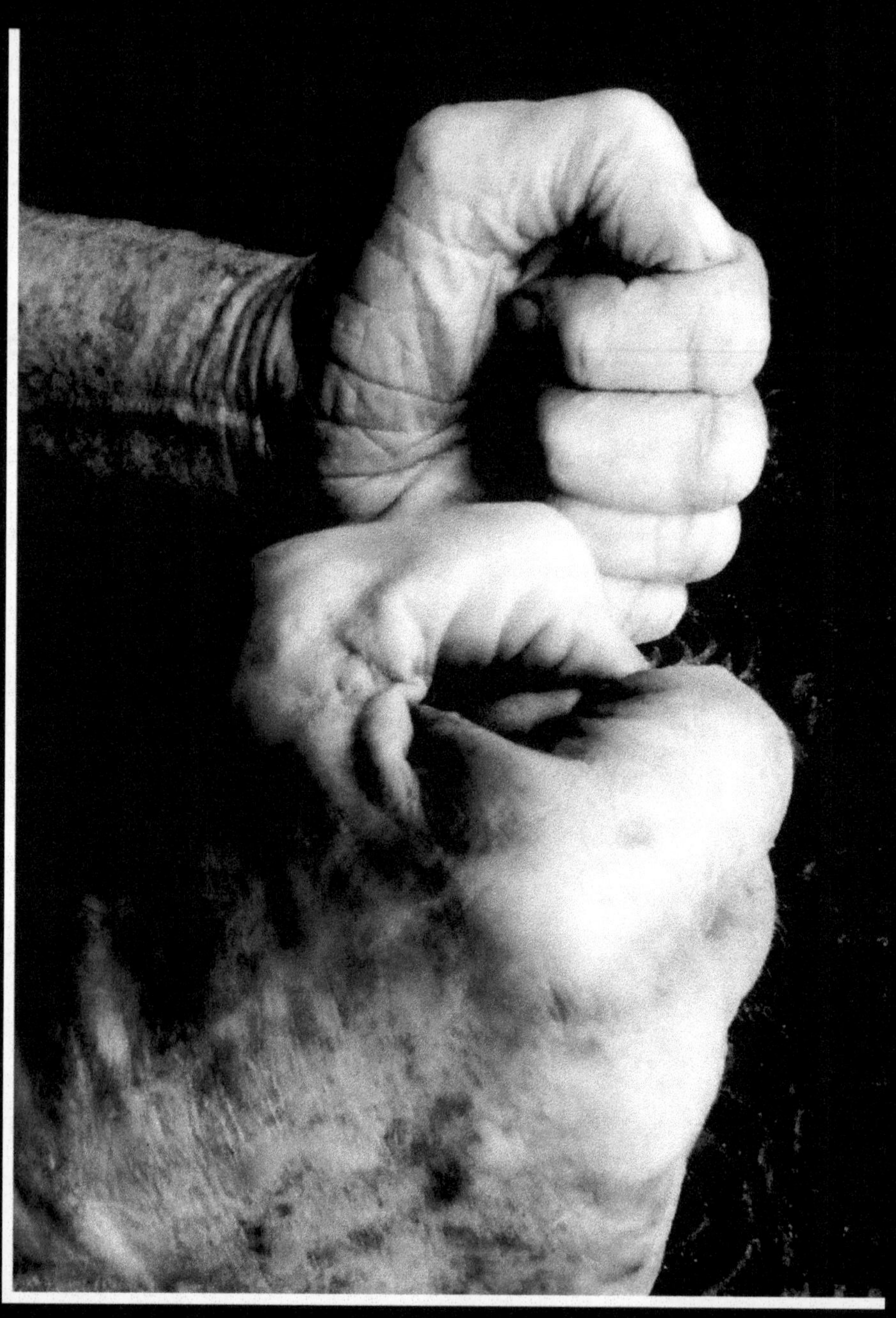

*"If you cut ten tonnes of cane a day,
you'd have to throw that ten tonnes into the carriages."*

I came from Ireland and it took a long time to get used to the steaming heat and humidity up here. It was seasonal work, so you worked long hard days to get your quota. You got paid by the weight of the cane you cut, so you worked hard and made the most of it while it lasted.

I cut sugarcane from Ingham to Mossman for sixteen seasons. I began working in a gang, then found out some men were not pulling their weight. So I began working in pairs with men who worked as hard as me. We could cut up to twelve tonne of cane each day. On one contract we worked 72 hours without sleep and just a few short breaks to eat and drink.

Our hands would be covered in blisters at the beginning of each season. The sweat on our hands would make the handle slip. Some men would urinate on their blisters and hands to 'toughen them up'. I'm not sure if it really worked, but you give anything a go so you can turn up and work the next day.

After you cut the cane, you bundle the cane stalks ready to be railed out of the farm. Heaving up the heavy bundles into the open carriages of the cane trains and pile the bundles almost as high as the carriages. Then you throw thick chains over the whole lot to tie it all down. If you cut 10 tonne of cane a day, you would have to throw that 10 tonne into the carriages. It was back breaking work, but it paid well the harder you worked.

***"Look, my hands are like a woman's hands, all soft.
They used to be hard, covered in callouses and blisters when I was working."***

I came to Australia when I was 18 years old to make a life. Back then people were scared of me, coming from another country, speaking another language. It was hard to meet girls. It took me six months to learn basic English just to communicate with other workers.

You had to be versatile. I worked on a cattle station in the Northern Territory for a while. Then I settled down in Ingham cutting sugarcane. Cutting cane all day from sunrise, finishing at 7-8 or 9pm at night 7 days a week for the whole season.

It was seasonal work, you cut cane from farm to farm for about 100 days a year. Then you looked for other work. At the end of each cane season, I went south to the Riverina area by train to pick peaches, apricots and grapes. Working 6 ½ days a week 12-15 hours a day. I could pick 3 tonne of fruit a day, a few hundred buckets.

*Young single men's greatest assets were their hands and their ability to work hard.
They knew little of Australia and had to overcome many hurdles.
Yet, they knew they could make good money if they worked hard and ultimately
be able to build a future in this new country.*

## My journey took me to Cape Tribulation, Far North Queensland...

Cape Tribulation in Far North Queensland is a remote wilderness in the World Heritage rainforest of the Daintree National Park. It's the only place in the world here two giant World Heritage sites meet each other, the Wet Tropics and the Great Barrier Reef.

The dense, tropical mountain rainforest pours onto the sandy beaches of the Coral Sea in a forceful tug of war for boundaries. Monsoonal troughs brings about 2010mm of rain each year, flooding all in sight. The extreme humidity in summer is oppressive, your skin is constantly damp.

Most people know that the Great Barrier Reef is the largest living natural coral reef ecosystem on earth. Yet few know about much about the unique Daintree Rainforest. It's estimated to be 135-180 million years old making it one of oldest rainforests on the planet. What makes this so remarkable, is that it's a living museum. Cataloguing an almost complete record in the evolution of plant life on our planet, unlike anywhere in the world. It's also filled with a bizarre number of distinctive, weird and wonderful creatures.

The first road to Cape Tribulation was cleared only in 1962. Previously, access to all northern settlements was only by boat or barge through crocodile infested waters. Not too much has changed. Today, you take the small vehicle ferry across the Daintree River and immediately you are driving through the rainforest engulfing you by its thick canopy. You feel as if you have stepped back into a time long before human existence.

The scenery is lush and wildly raw. You hear the silence of the rainforest as it begins to close around you. Evolutionary crocodiles lurk in the waters and huge flightless Cassowaries, with razor sharp, dagger shaped claws stroll along the side of the road. The ever-growing rainforest swallows abandoned buildings as nature and wildlife quickly regains their space. It's a magnificent, forceful rainforest that man cannot tame, reminding us that we are mere guests in nature.

With the oppressive summer humidity, there is little relief to cool off as swimming in the ocean and waterways is completely out of the question. Large danger signs dot the beaches warning you of crocodiles and deadly seasonal jellyfish. Exotic tropical fruit orchards and organic tea plantations grow in the rich, alluvial soils. It makes for a thrilling, spectacular visit. Only some have managed to make this home.

Not far from here, I met a delightful gentleman named Pat whose family were pioneers to the Daintree, being the first white people to settle in the area in 1932. Pat's eyesight is failing, yet his mind is sharp of his memories and stories.

It was and still is a harsh and challenging environment to create a settlement or any type of farming. Yet one family persisted with various endeavours over the years including farming, timber cutting and cattle. The ever moving rainforest had the upper hand and won over many times. One great challenge was transport. With no roads in the early years everything had to be shipped in and out by boat. It was quite an isolating life as the boat only stopped in Cape Tribulation once a week on its way to Cooktown in the north.

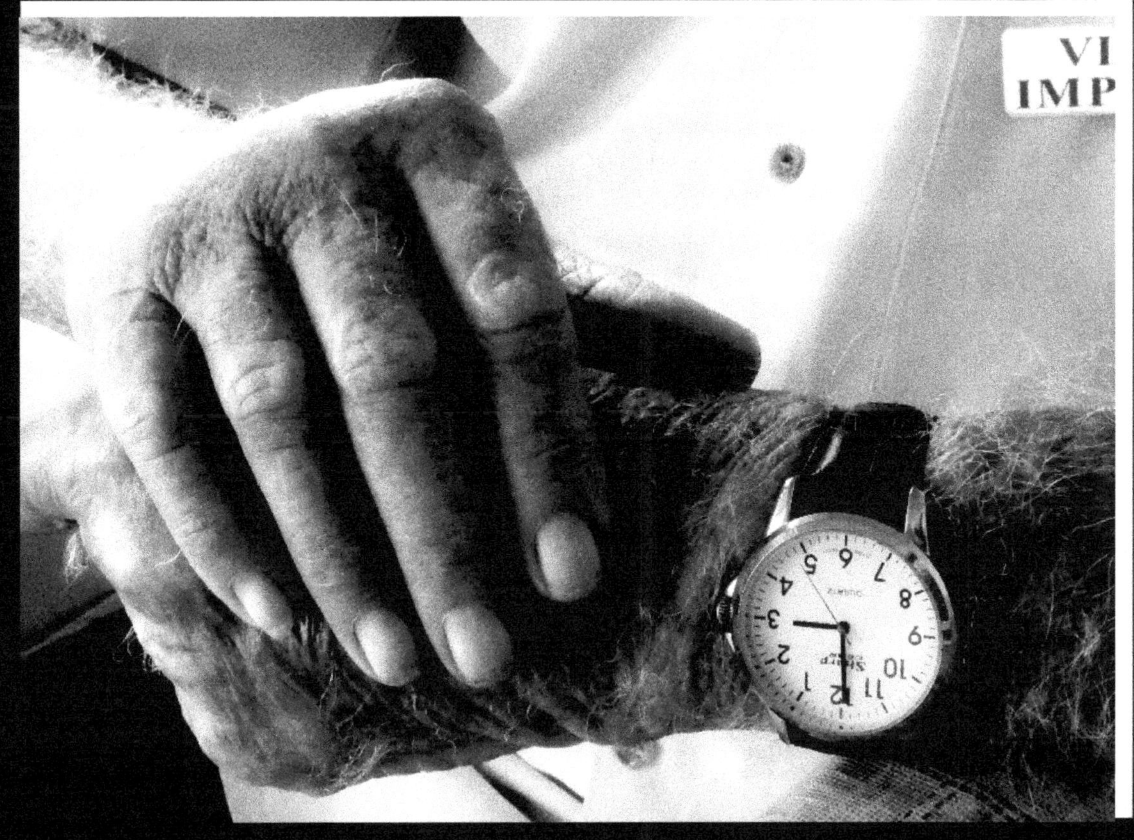


*'I was always clearing virgin land, to build plantations or homes.'*

*"I was always clearing virgin land, to build plantations or homes."*

I was born in Cairns and worked in my parents shop when I was a kid. The family also had five acres of land in The Daintree. We cleared the land to plant bananas.

I began working as an apprentice carpenter at age 13 years to get a trade.

You were a man at the age of 16 back then. You worked alongside seasoned older men and were expected to work like them.

Dad also cut red cedar and pencil pine trees. He freighted them to Thursday Island and Sydney by boat. The logs were sold, but the agent stole all the money. Two years of hard work gone. He lost everything, it nearly broke him. He wouldn't accept any handouts from the government or other people, he had too much pride. So he began to work again.

I went back to Cape Tribulation and cleared 160 acres of land for planting bananas and grazing cattle. Then I cleared another block. It was back breaking work, especially moving the large rocks. I cleared the land using an axe, cross saw and gelignite to break up the large rocks. There were no tractors back then.

Later, I bought a block of land with a sugarcane permit of 100 acres. Another block to be cleared. When the cane grew I cut it all by hand and shoulder loaded the bundles.

I alternated working on the cane farm and building homes for people in other areas in Australia. I worked seven days a week for three years. My wife and I even picked fruit for a few seasons in between building homes and looking after the cane farm.

Another time, I built houses and tobacco barns for two years. We moved around Australia quite a lot in those early years. I was always clearing virgin land to build plantations or houses.

After many years, I bought back my father's farm at Cape Tribulation and built another home, this time for the family.

Many people had looked for a track to be able to build a road from Cape Tribulation to Bloomfield to attract people to the area. Yet no one could not find a suitable track through the rainforest. Some friends and I walked through the bush to find a way, we found a way and a road was cleared to Bloomfield, then later to Cooktown.

*Many of the pristine farms and plantations we see today were created by clearing large tracks of virgin land by hand. Removing trees, scrub and large boulders. They were the pioneers of the land.*

## Striking gold in Hill End, New South Wales...

Hill End is an artist's dream for its historical timber buildings, rusted corrugated iron roofs, 100 year old lichen covered crooked fences and fragments of the past. Surrounded by rolling hills and fog filled valleys. Arriving on a bitterly cold winter's afternoon, I was second guessing if this was a good idea to visit Hill End in winter.

My campervan had zero insulation, so you do what it takes to keep warm. I double socked and multi layered for the approaching night. Just as I settled in I heard what I thought was soft rain falling on my roof. Stepping out of my van in the morning, I found it hadn't rained. Instead, the landscape was blanketed in snow. Almost forgetting the freezing temperature, I quickly grabbed my camera and began capturing the scenery before the snow melted. I could see why it was an artist delight.

Nestled in a gully on top of a range, the area around Hill End began as pastoral land. Then in the 1850's gold was discovered and squatters moved in creating the tent town of Hill End. Its reputation as a gold mining town quickly spread when the world's largest single gold specimen was unearthed, the Holtermann Nugget. Weighing in at a whopping 630lb, this rock contained an estimated 3,000 ounces of gold and stood almost as tall as a man at 1.5metres high.

At the town's height, over 8,000 people lived in the area. The town itself was relatively compact and small in area, crammed with town services including 51 licenced hotels. Today, the town is an historic site with a population around 80 people and only one hotel remains standing.

It's a fascinating town steeped in history where the local kangaroo residents seems to outnumber the human residents. You find the large grey kangaroos lying or feeding around the town in the vacant blocks of land, campgrounds or residents and establishment's yards.

Plaques with images have been placed around the town where historic buildings once stood to give you an idea of what the town looked like in its heyday. Hearing that some people come to Hill End for a 'Pub Crawl'. What they do, is carry their filled eskies around the town and stop at each place where the pubs once stood. They'd have a drink then walk to the next site where a pub once stood in the day. A fun and sensible Pub Crawl!

Gold was still being panned long after the height of the mining era. It was a bit of a long shot if any old prospectors still lived in the area. Asking at the information centre and of course the only pub in town was to no avail. However, I did find a lady in her eighties who grew up in the area.

Betty lived in a charming cottage in the township. She was an effervescent lady who described a simple, wholesome life of connectedness with family, community and life. Betty retold her story with such fondness for her childhood. Each member of the family had jobs around the home and the food was fresh which they grew or caught, a seemingly idyllic, simplistic lifestyle.

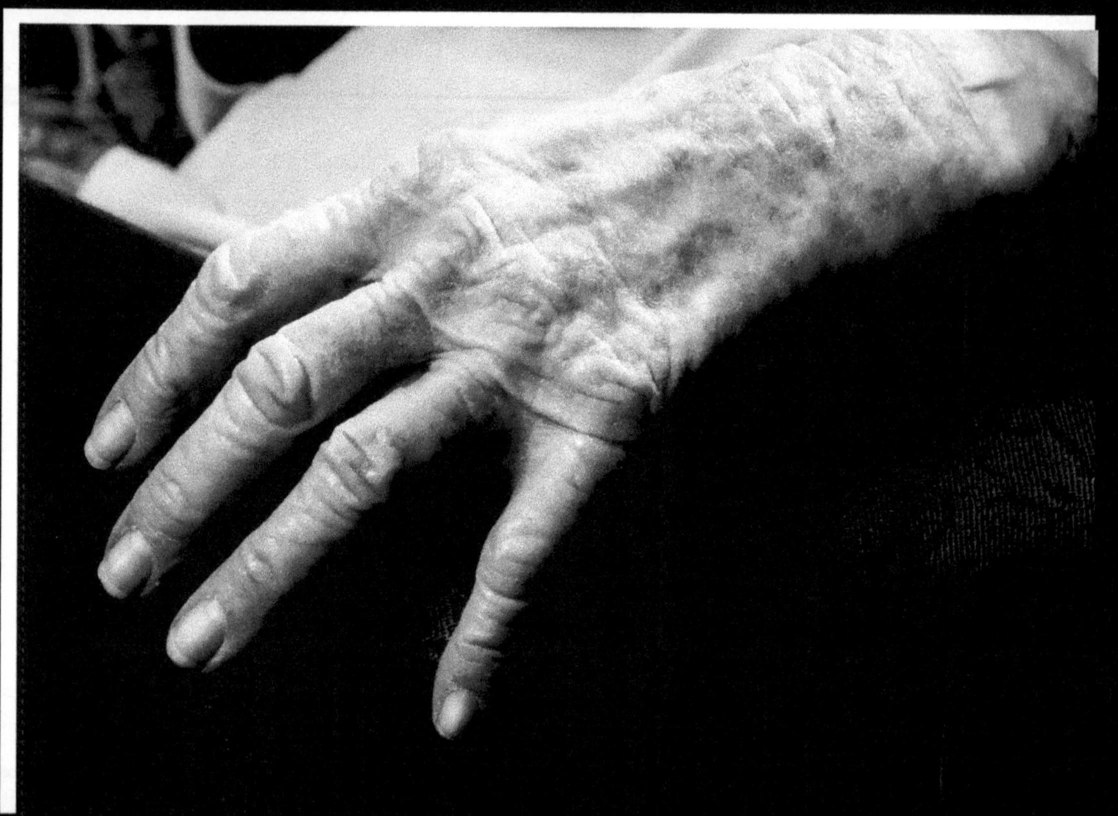

*'When I was twelve,
I began killing rabbits for food.'*

*"When I was twelve,*
*I was killing and skinning rabbits for food."*

I was the eldest child in the family, so I looked after the babies while mum did chores around the house.

We had no radio or television, so we talked to each other a lot at night, we knew what was going on in the family, with our neighbours and the town.

We didn't have to go to the store for a lot of our food as we grew our own fruits and vegetables and we had chickens for eggs and their meat. We didn't buy much beef, it was expensive.

I'd milk the cows each day and we made our own butter. It was a lot of fun to knock off bee hives and rob their honey to eat.

I began cooking when I was very young. I began making jam and pies from the fruit we grew and baked cakes and biscuits. When I got older I made roasts and stews for the family.

When I was twelve years old, I began to kill rabbits. I trapped them, cracked their necks, skinned them, cut them up and cooked them for dinner. I killed chooks too, cut their heads off with an axe, pluck them, stuff them and cook them.

I helped my dad cut tree logs for fire wood using a cross saw. Dad was very fast and it was hard to keep up most of the time. (Laughing)

The work I did when I was young was hard, but it was an awful lot of fun!

All the cooking I did when I was young created my great love for cooking and stayed with me all my life. I still bake cakes for visitors and stalls in Hill End. Good old fashioned country cooking. I even cooked with Maggie Beer a few times when I was an adult.

*Life in country towns was a simple. Most people were semi self-sufficient.*
*Growing their own fruit and vegetables and raising animals.*
*Most had no electricity. Using wood fired stoves and kerosene lamps.*
*Water tanks provided their water. They say they had more family time.*
*Children took on responsibilities around the home at an early age.*

# One day you will regret not asking

Whilst visiting my mother in a nursing home in her final years, I had a wonderful opportunity to meet several residents in the building. On each visit, I found it incredibly sad that so many residents rarely or didn't receive visitors. The staff were wonderful, nurturing and caring, yet it wasn't family, their family who they cared for over many decades. I wondered when we moved away from valuing and respecting our elders and their knowledge. They now appear to be discarded from this fast paced society, yet their stories, their history is rich and full, when you took the time to listen.

One resident was a cracker of a lady called Mary who was well into her nineties. She was bound to a wheel chair as her body had failed her. She was hysterically funny with a sharp, quick mind possessing an upbeat positive attitude to life. Current with a broad range of news, she loved to have a chat or two discussing what was happening in the world. She had seen a multitude of changes through her life. Mary was born in Tasmania and had been a career nurse all her life.

One day, a lady walked towards the old piano in the dining room, placed her hands on the keys producing some semi recognisable chords. She paused for a moment, hands poised over the pianos keys, closed her eyes for a moment and took a deep breath. She opened her eyes and her fingers found the keys in perfect unison as the sweet sound of Debussy wafted through the room. It was a flawless performance with a beautiful controlled passion. I was mesmerised and will admit, a little teary.

A little while later, I sat in a chair beside her and expressed how much I enjoyed her piano playing. She looked at me and said; 'Oh I don't play the piano dear, I think my father did, yes, I used to sit on his lap as he played, but I don't play the piano.' I later found that she was a concert pianist in her younger years. She had remembered every single, perfectly timed note, yet fifteen mins later didn't remember she could play the piano. You have to wonder how does our spirit live or exist without a conscious memory. From that experience, I believe that it can and does. I'll wait for the experts to correct me with this.

There was a tall, sturdy gentleman bound to a wheelchair. When classical music played in the common lounge room, his upper body immediately ignited into action. His highly expressive arms, hands and fingers artistically floated through the air with such grace. His face was poised and proud. The music transported him to the stage of his youth, as the Russian ballet dancer.

Another gentleman had a huge poster hung in his room of a muscle bound man in his prime. Whenever he walked into his room, he would stop and stare at the poster with a huge knowing smile. This image obviously made him happy for some reason. I was to learn, this poster was of himself in his younger years as a professional boxer.

**Oh the stories these people must possess. There is a multitude of history just waiting to be heard. Before it's too late, capture and record your own family's stories.**

**One day you will regret not asking, then your own history will be lost to time.**

*'I loved being a nurse,*
*but there were a lot of dirty jobs.'*

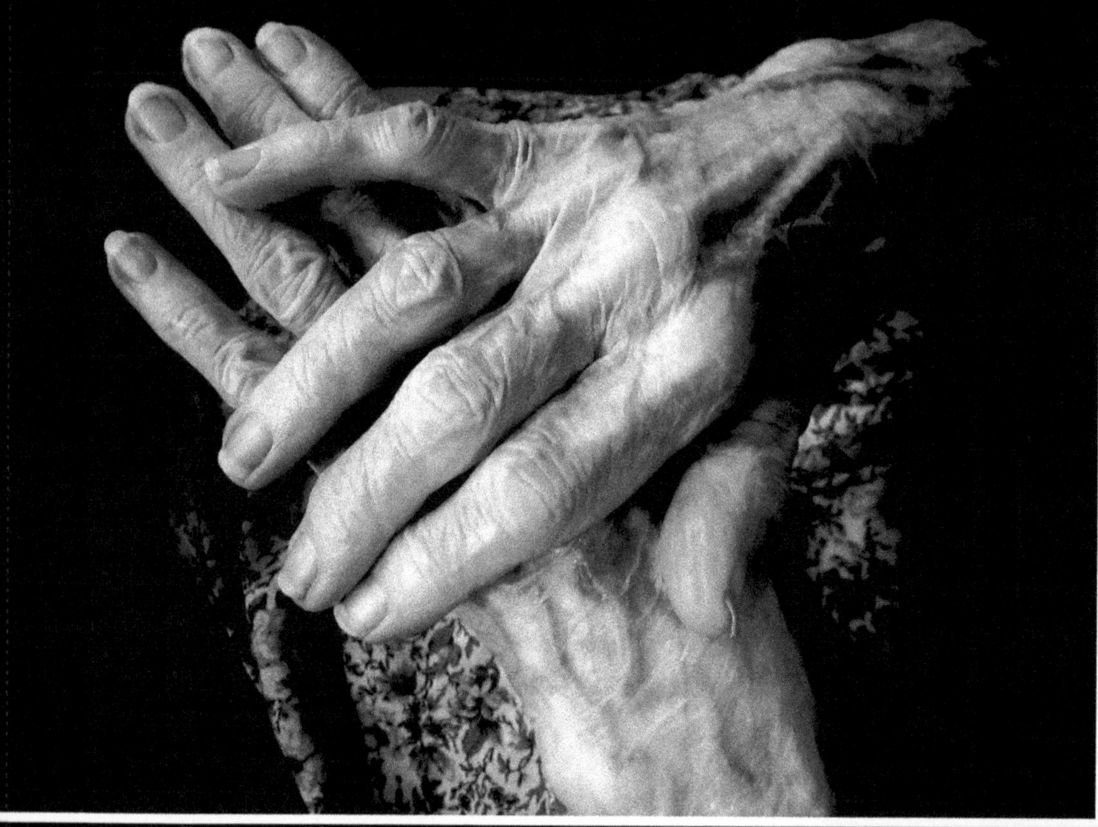

*"I loved being a nurse,
but there were a lot of dirty jobs."*

Nursing changed a lot over my lifetime, but the basics didn't.

I was a no fuss nurse. I didn't like to mollycoddle patients too much. I would joke and laugh with the patients. It was better that they didn't dwell on their ailments and focus on getting well and going home. That's how we did it.

We didn't wear gloves back then so our hands were into everything. Changing bedpans, cleaning up bile, vomit, human faeces, blood. You had to bathe their open wounds, oh you know, all the dirty stuff. We'd just wash our hands and get back to work. But that was our job, it had to be done, so you didn't think about it.

Our uniforms were white starched stiff dresses, they had to be clean all the time. We wore aprons with bibs, to protect our dress. So we would change the apron if it got dirty and so we didn't spread any disease. We wore those silly little starched hats that didn't do anything other than look pretty. We had to wear white lace up shoes and stockings. The uniforms changed over the years and became more practical and relaxed.

Nursing in the war was very different. A good friend told me that you had to put your emotions to one side and just do your job. You had to nurse those poor bastards the best you could in the conditions. Those men had some really horrible wounds and many men died. It was very sad, but you couldn't let it get to you too much because you had other men to nurse and had to be positive. Sometimes they didn't have enough supplies to dress their wounds properly. So you had to make do and hope new supplies would arrive soon.

You didn't think too much about what was going on in the war or it would make you mad. You just kept doing your job. Fix them up to go home or back to the fighting. That's why we were there. Our job was easier than what the soldiers had to do. I think that's how you got through the war.

I loved being a nurse, helping people, there were always a lot of dirty jobs, but someone had to do them. (laughing)

*Nurses have a vital role in healing the sick and wounded.
In the early days of Australia, nursing duties were carried out by convicts
who had no training. Hygiene wasn't even considered.*

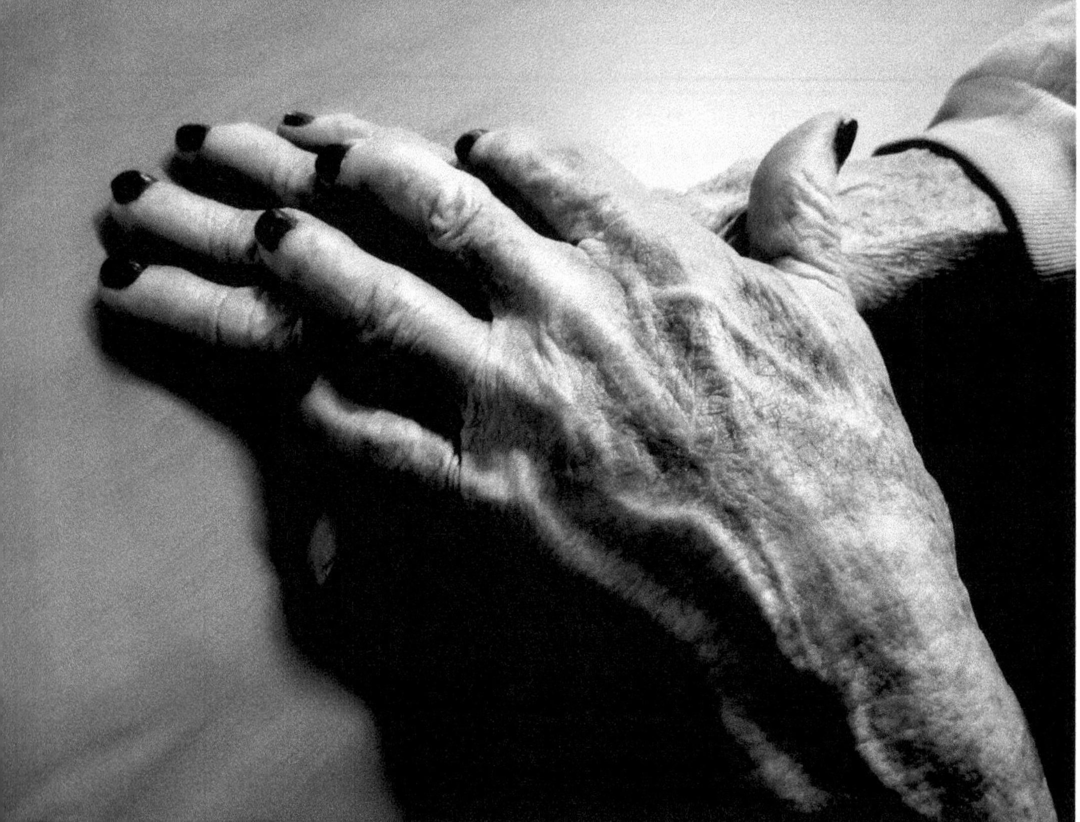

*"Idle hands make mischief."*

Busy, busy, busy hands all day long. Mothers from this era somehow appeared to have studied the same mythical Common Sense Mothers handbook. Just talk to any of their children across the country and you will hear almost identical stories about how they ran their household and reared their children.

The heartbeat of the family and home, mothers were the silent force fusing the family together while systematically and silently juggling multiple daily chores with apparent ease. They were part of the family's every waking moment and ready to jump to every sound in the darkness of the night. Their work never ceased.

Blessed with gentle loving hands to cradle their babies and caress their children when they were sick. Yet quick hands to sting a slap on your backside as they watched you through eyes at the back of their head.

They instinctively knew how to be economical from their recollections of The Depression and rationing during the war, nothing was wasted. They could creatively make something, anything out of mere scraps.

Every morsel of food her family ate was lovingly touched by kneading, mixing, peeling, dicing, cutting and folding with her hands. Magically creating three meals a day with the simplest and barest of ingredients. Stretching food for unexpected visitors at meal time.

Housework was manual, sweeping floors, dusting, beating dirt from floor rugs. Scrubbing everything in sight with good old fashioned elbow grease and harsh soaps. Labouriously washing clothes using a washing board then pegging them on a line in the sun to dry, more folding.

Mothers could mend a hole in your sock, hand sew a dress or knit you a cardigan from odds and ends. When you outgrew your clothes, they could add wide a hem or seam to make it last for another few years or unravel that cardigan and re knit it to your size.

They washed your body and cut your hair. Bathed your wounds without a fuss, gave you a reassuring hug and sent you back out to play.

They believed that idle hands made mischief and put you to work whenever you whined that you were bored. So you learnt to keep busy - just like her.

Many households had a vegetable garden and raised chooks that needed attention. Some mothers took up the slack on farms – all the while juggling their daily chores with ease and in silence.

Busy, busy hands. Their hands possessed a strong work ethic and knew how to be busy all day long, year after year, decade after decade – and yet they never wore out.

Mothers were the heart and soul of the family that tied the family together, that was their role.

## What did I get from this journey

Oh phew! How and where do you begin to explain the multitude of gifts you take away from any kind of journey? The list is long and some things just can't be defined or put into words.

What you 'learn' covers a very broad spectrum. Every day was a continual classroom of discovery and working out all the 'how' situations. The constant movement heightens your awareness of your surrounds mentally and physically. I'm now more equipped to tackle future adventures and projects with the vast knowledge I've gained. Creating a stronger confidence to set out again into the unknown with a mere idea. Recognising that persistence pays off by knowing if you ask a multitude of people or even asking yourself questions that it will take you to your outcome, eventually. Finding ways to get around my own limitations. I'd also realised there is more to life than pointlessly running on a mouse wheel type existence. It exposed a host of options to live a happy, fulfilled life - when you dare to take the steps.

My views of the world and cultures broadened from conversations with the many international people who travel around our country. My views on life expanded from speaking with people from a broad range of generations. Any journey taxes you physically, mentally and emotionally. You can travel in a variety of ways, yet I found the simpler, the better. With less distractions, it creates more attention to the reason you are travelling. I'd also learnt the huge difference between 'travelling' to 'taking a holiday'.

Discovering a less artificial life where introducing yourself (via your name) held little to no significance in conversations with fellow travellers. Nor was there any shame or notice that you were still wearing the same clothes from 3 days ago. What was important were the experiences and places you had witnessed. So was the natural flow of sharing and helping each other, without an expected exchange. It didn't matter that you may never see these travellers again, it was just an open connection in that moment. People didn't seem to judge you by material things, your job, status, where you lived, what vehicle you drove. It didn't matter that I wasn't wearing make-up, that my hair was badly needing a cut or that my shoes weren't clean. This was a far cry from a city life. I know this may sounds like a clique, but it was what was inside a person, their openness, joyful personality, stories of their travels and making a human connection that truly mattered.

Finally understanding that thread of who we are as Australians. How our identity evolved and what made up our heritage. How we, as Australians are so fortunate to be living on this isolated continent. Learning about the fascinating aspects of our history, at times first hand. The list of what I have gained is endless. The only thing I lost was living an unfulfilled life.

This journey has created an avid yearning to learn more about our Indigenous history, their culture and their stories. To 'try' to learn what it really means to belong to the land. I really don't know if my own fleeting glimpses are comparable in any way.

It's also difficult to fully express how deeply privileged I was to have met and hear stories from this remarkable generation. Many times, I was humbled by their stories of resilience and their simplistic, yet powerful attitude to life and work. How they made an existence in some of the most unforgiving areas of Australia astounded me time and again. Undoubtedly, there will never be another generation of their like.

Too often, I felt a tinge of embarrassment for being one of the 'soft and privileged' generations. In an odd way, I envied what this generation endured and achieved in their uncomplicated, yet physically challenging life. There appeared to be a silent satisfaction of a life well lived and a feeling of contribution to something larger than themselves. Is that how we measure life? I wonder if I will I be as content with my own life endeavours when I reach their age? I can only wait and see.

Learning different aspects of our harsh history provided a boundless admiration for our prior generations. With a deep appreciation and gratitude for creating this strong foundation in our amazing country. There was a sense I was witnessing a part of our history that was coming to an close, which saddened me at times. However, the overall feeling was euphoric that I was strangely involved in a living piece of history. In an odd way, it felt like time travel.

In between my searches of these people and the endless researching, I focused on the land itself in a personal intimate way, through the lens of my camera. Viewing life through a lens draws your attention to the details of compelling forms, textures, colour and the beauty in the harshness. Your eyes and mind are continuously scanning your surrounds with a greater purpose, singling out an element which portrays a subject. By photo journaling this trip with tens of thousands of images as a record of the features which make up this diverse land allowed me to understand it more intimately and through the eyes of innocent wonder. You never really feel alone when you travel with a camera.

Unashamedly, I fell deeply in love with this land we call home. The diversity of landscapes across Australia is outstanding. Every aspect of our vast countryside continuously stole my heart. However, the iconic Outback touched my soul and left me speechless again and again with its gift of vibrant, stark raw scenery, infinite blue skies and the inner peace this ancient land imparts on your soul.

On a number of occasions, I left my camera gear in my backpack just sitting for hours absorbing the landscape's essence. They were incredibly personal moments that I didn't want to share with anyone, not even my camera. To this day, I won't express those scenes to another soul, they just sit inside of myself. Those precious moments made me feel small and insignificant in the scheme of time and space, stripping away your ego - yet made me feel whole.

This book was always intended to be about the people who created our heritage, and still is. However my thoughts kept drawing me back to the land itself.

***This beautiful, brutal land forced generations of people to do extraordinary things to survive, create an existence and a nation.***

***Without acknowledging the collective elements of this land, our heritage would be an entirely different set of stories.***

***And so...The people and the land became one.***

# Gift of a Heritage

It all began when our continent drifted into an isolated part on this globe, slowly shaping and re shaping the landscape. Tens of millions of years later, a unique series of events, circumstances and attitudes created our current heritage. Inheriting a solid foundation is a generous, valuable gift. Our convicts, early settlers and the following few generations formed a proud and strong identity, traits which characterise Australia as a whole.

The foundation of modern Australia was carved over a few short generations by the hands of many men, women, and children from a multitude of nationalities. Bold people who made the most with what was in front of them in an unfamiliar land filled with great obstacles and setbacks. Through pioneering, perseverance and ingenuity, they shaped successful pastoral, agricultural, mining and many more industries in less than 200 years. Australia became one of the largest food producers and exporters in the world out of the most arid habitable continent on our planet. It wasn't an easy journey for anyone, yet they did it, achieved it.

Australia can now proudly meet its own internal needs as well as cover the needs to many countries around the world from its natural resources and food productivity. Without the pioneering, tenacity and boldness of these few generations, Australia would not be in this envied position today. They set a high benchmark of hard work and ingenuity to emulate.

Australia is certainly not perfect. Yet in comparison, we live in a reasonably politically stable and 'safe' country. I've often wondered, what sort of country would we be living in if our defenders didn't put their lives on the line time and again to protect not just this land, but our values, our way of life? Hearing the philosophical words from an elderly WWII digger; 'If we didn't fight over there, there wouldn't be a here.' A deep sense of gratitude rushed over me of their committed, selfless sacrifice for our 'home' and way of life for future generations.

Our often over looked inventors and scientists use that resilient innovative spirit to continue to produce major contributions to the world in many fields. Such contributions save and enhance millions of lives worldwide. The traits of our deep love of the outdoors, hard work and fair play has produced many world class athletes and sports people. Our actors and business people are sought out internationally for their humour, classless and grounded work ethics. Yes, we owe a lot to our early generations and their humble beginnings on many levels.

Were these first 200 years perfect? Absolutely not. By taking an honest look at our warts and all history allows us to navigate the future with more confidence. Learning and understanding what it took for our country to be in this sought-after position.

Correcting the mistakes and ignorance, then building on our strengths can take us into a brighter and more confident future.

The period of building Australia's foundation is at an end. We are at the beginning of another journey, a new era is emerging while holding onto a remarkable, solid gift. I wonder what sort of legacy we will hand over to our future generations.

***I often hear our younger generation say that the future is too uncertain. But is it really that uncertain?***

# Change is a certainty

Debating which generation's life was better or worse would be futile. Each generation has their own unique set of challenges, both personally and globally. The common thread is that each generation sets out into an unknown future, filled with unseen opportunities and blinded enthusiasm. Only one thing in life is certain - change is constant.

I often hear despair from our younger generations saying they believe the world and their future is too uncertain. With the constant bombardment of doom and gloom world news at their fingertips I can see why they may believe this. But is the amount of uncertainty really so different to prior generations?

Did any of our prior generations really know what their future would hold, how they would have to navigate their life and overcome the numerous trials? I doubt it. This Silent Generation had their fair share of major challenging situations to overcome. They were born around The Depression era where a meal of bread and dripping was commonplace. Did they know if the Depression would continue throughout their entire lives? Or did our defenders know if they would return home alive from a devastating world war where around 30,000 Australians had died? How could they possibly foresee the dramatic technology changes of the 1950's and 1960's? Could they envision transport changing from horseback to man on the moon? Or communicating with hand written letters to the mind blowing era of instant messaging via emails, text messages or Skype? When will we reach the stage of 'beam me up!' technology?

Yet each generation overcame their challenges and accepted the changes one step at a time. The most important thing they did was keep moving forward in spite of the apparent lack of certainty in life. They didn't give up, finding creative ways around the many hurdles.

Each generation has its turn to make its mark in the world and to leave their own legacy. By understanding our past and the trials from individual's stories, they help steer our own future, both personally and globally. By listening to their revealing stories, they give you a reference and confidence that others have gone through life and made it to the end. Learning from prior mistakes and adding to the strengths to continue the cycle in spite of a perceived unknown future.

I wonder if our future generations will be as surprised when changes occur in their lifetime as with the Silent Generation's era. Imagination, knowledge and technology have shown us endless possibilities rather than uncertainty. Will anything that technology creates truly surprise us again?

The defining moment of possibilities for me came when I watched Neil Armstrong set foot on the moon. The entire world paused in that moment in absolute awe and partial disbelief that mankind could achieve something so astonishing. Yet there we were watching the conclusion of a bold idea. 'That's one small step for man, one giant leap for mankind'. We can now see and expect space travel to be part of our future. How quickly our expectations of possibilities can change

***Imagination sets us off in a direction,<br>we just need to keep taking steps into each unknown.***

## Seize opportunities in spite of the unknown

For my own journey of discovery, all I had was a simple idea and a few weeks to set the wheels in motion. Having absolutely no idea how I was going to achieve my objective, how to go about it or what would develop from these stories. I hadn't even contemplated what I would learn about our country or how it would change my thinking or my life. All I had to do was fumble and move in the direction step by step. New avenues of thoughts and ideas opened up from speaking to thousands of people along the way. Having an insatiable curiosity kept me on track.

Fortunately, I didn't give myself time to think of the details or plan the journey. If I did, it would have seemed insurmountable to execute and it never would have happened. Swapping high heels and a city life for boots and a transient journey into remote areas of Australia, took me well out of my comfort zone. Learning the logistics of living 'on the road' in a small campervan was a major stretch and a huge learning curve. I just had to seize the opportunity in spite of the unknown.

Only now can I sit back and reflect on where this journey took me and how it evolved. Showing where each action led me to the next stage in a seemingly orchestrated unknown plan. Although this 'invisible plan' only presented itself at the end of the journey.

If I didn't seize this opportunity and continued to live a predictable city life, I would have ignored and missed an extraordinary experience to enrich and change my life.

In the first few months of this journey, all I had was uncertainty and an outpouring of 'where' questions. Having no idea where I would find these people. Where to find water each day and the luxury of a real shower. Where I was going to pull over each night to sleep, let alone where I'd be in six months or that magical corporate question 'where will you be in five years'. For me, it was, 'where do I go from here'. You just keep moving forward until you see a change of certainty. Certain that your actions have traction and will lead you to your end goal.

It took me eight months to comprehend the workings of amps and watts for my power supply of two house batteries. Many people on the way patiently explained and yet my mind was still blank. Even Google didn't help me understand. Obviously I learnt the hard way when I had completely destroyed both batteries power capacity. Only then did I finally begin to understand. I was and still am totally unskilled in the mechanical or fixer her up fields. My tool box consisted of a roll of duct tape, six ockie straps, a set of four $2 screw drivers, and a small hammer, however it didn't deter me to not to continue. I would learn somehow, even if it was going to be the hard ways.

This whole journey posed never ending questions. In time, the daily 'where' questions were quickly answered, morphing into endless 'what, how and why' questions.

What did these stories and people have in common...What was the driving force of this generation...What were their values...What were the defining elements that formed our heritage...How was our identity moulded...Why was our land so unique, how was it created. The list of questions went on and on. Driving me to research deeper, exposing fascinating facts.

I'd learnt more during these relatively few short years, than I had in decades. I was in my element. From a very young age I was the annoying 'why' child, continuously asking questions with an added 'but why?' when I received answers. This drove my parents crazy at times. To tell you the truth, it perplexed me many times for the need to know or try to understand why throughout life

This journey stretched me mentally and physically. At times it was draining. However, I took frequent breaks by hiking and exploring breathtaking areas of our country while photographing the diverse landscapes and iconic sights.

During the last year all the discomforts, aggravations and a few scary situations of the physical journey had now funnily morphed into comical tales and I had a semi solid vision for this book. This journey was winding down. The continual questions had eased...it was a matter of connecting everything I had learned and experienced into one idea.

If I hadn't seized this opportunity, I would have overlooked an incredibly rewarding experience. Depriving myself of an amazing opportunity to grow and learn. I would have missed witnessing Australia's incredible landscapes and learning about our history from people who were still alive. The chance to meet an incredible array of people from all walks of life and those who were on their own personal journey would have been lost.

I had exchanged a limited life for an expansive life. The journey opened up new attitudes and more prospects for my future. Isn't that our purpose by nature – to learn and grow?

Another thought puzzled me at times, and that was our relationship with technology.

***Our purpose by nature is to learn and grow.***

***To challenge your current status and explore new ideas.***

***The cycle of change continues.***

# Our relationship with technology

Technology has certainly enhanced the quality of our lives in many ways and I for one am thankful for much of it. Finding just how much technology we really need was becoming a bit of a challenge.

Listening to numerous life stories from a broad range of age groups, I was always aware to notice how different generations viewed life with common threads. One noticeable change I didn't expect was a general shift from people who were born a mere ten years or so later than my specific targeted group of people.

They were too young to participate in WWII and found themselves thrust into the era of technology of the 50's and 60's. A large percentage of their working life centred on machinery and I found the retelling of their life stories were noticeably different.

The stories tended to be aimed on status, money, what they accumulated rather than any life endeavours. The smiles, laughter and pride were mostly absent, so were the stories of real obstacles, hardships and community. Talk of that profound deep bond of mateship appeared diluted or lacking. Perhaps they didn't know what it meant to 'battle' with life as in The Depression or WWII to appreciate life itself or what they already possessed. I wasn't sure if that had any correlation to their stories, yet my mind wanted to explore the likelihoods.

Many of this group's stories began when they were at the height of their career with, "Well I was a foreman to over 50 people..." "I was driving the largest..." A good number didn't mention their younger years or their parents influence growing up. Ego and blame crept in as to why their life could have been different. That strong acceptance to life from the earlier generation was mainly absent. Understand, this was a generalisation from my experiences and didn't apply to everyone. Yet the difference was quite obvious with a consistent thread in these conversations.

It didn't take long to work out how they were different, but it did take a while to work out why they were different. The word ego kept jumping to mind. There was a lingering sense of trying to impress rather than that casual matter of fact style of retelling their stories. Also appearing was a strong emphasise on the types of machinery they used for work, rather than any personal endeavours. Talk of the monetary value of their homes and their wages was also present. I wondered what effect technology had on our lives, our core spirit.

When travelling, you get to see all kinds of modes of transport. From bicycles to basic campervans, 20 year old vehicles to state of the art luxurious motorhomes, caravans and hi-tech computerised 4WD's. Interestingly, I'd seen many state of the art vehicles with every conceivable convenience stop dead in their tracks by a technical computer error, having to be towed to the nearest specialised dealer to be fixed. On the flip side, I'd seen people creatively repair older vehicles with makeshift items and off they go again.

I found the people who used simpler modes of transport had by far more fascinating tales and tended to explore more unique places. They weren't afraid to collect a few scratches and dents on their vehicles or wear the many discomforts and inconveniences in the pursuit of adventure and experiences.

***It appeared that the explosive wave of technology in our lives altered us in some ways and it wasn't always for our own good.***

For a good proportion of this journey, connection to my outside world was restricted to local radio stations where I learnt what was going on around my immediate space. The complexity of the fast flash headlines of doom world news was gone. Television was non-existent and Wi-Fi connection was spasmodic to nil in remote areas, eliminating wasting time on social media. It was refreshing by removing that constant bombardment of technology for prolonged periods. In ways, this ignorance was pure bliss. It freed me up to spend more time speaking face to face with real people and focus on things that was important to me. I do want to know what is happening in the world and the issues we face. However, I didn't need or want it in my life on a daily basis.

I looked back to my city life. People rushing around constantly looking down at their mobile phones, texting, checking their social media and playing with their hundreds of apps. It didn't appear so unusual at the time, but now I see it as pure insanity. We are missing the immense vibrancy of life unfolding right in front of us and here we are spending our life anxiously buried in devices looking down.

***Our human spirit doesn't appear to be aligned or caught up to the speed that technology is evolving.***

We can already see an alarming percentage of young children with a wide variety of social and mental issues. The hefty amounts of time spent indoors on their phone, internet or watching television eats away at their human spirit.

In prior generations, we were simply told to go outside and play. We didn't have to ask what play meant, we instinctively knew. Our friends were living beings we could touch, physically make a connection, they weren't hundreds of indiscriminate names on a computer screen. We spoke with emotions, hearing the subtle tones in voices to understand their intent. Shorthand text messages creates anxiety as we think of a variety of scenarios to the words true meanings.

Play set us up for life using our imagination, developing social and negotiation skills – and having fun. Finding and extending our limits, gaining confidence. Creating real friends who will be there for you in times of need with a hug. Playing outside physically connects us with nature. We have so much land in our country to explore and most people don't utilise this amazing gift.

Many times during this trip, I juggled with the question of how much of our human spirit is deprived by today's highly mechanised world. Are we using technology to benefit our lives or are we becoming technology's slave, trapped to the wants of the latest 'toys' and time saving devices which are actually consuming more of our physical and mental time.

Speaking with this particular older generation made me wonder if humans are basically wired and happiest being in touch with the land in some way. Rather than an insular, comfortable life with all the modern conveniences at their fingertips. Technology has improved our lives in the science and commercial fields, but how much is too much in our everyday life?

***I needed to find my Goldilocks mid ground by combining the best of both worlds.***

# Finding the Goldilocks mid ground

My aim is to make technology work for me, rather than being its slave. My world didn't come crashing down when I eliminated a large proportion of technology. In fact I exchanged a limited life for an expansive life.

Travelling minimally gave me a bit of a head start to understand how technology affects us as humans. Right from the start, I made it a rule to take a month to decide if I really needed the current 'bright shiny new thing' I wanted. That gave me time to think if it was a need or a want and around 90% of the time they were unnecessary wants. These choices allowed me to travel to more out of the way places and spend more time both physically and mentally exploring with the least amount of effort. I didn't have to look after or burdened by 'things' and my limitations of personal space forced me to be 'outside' the majority of the time.

It will be a bit of a juggling act to find that Goldilocks mid ground with my own relationship to technology, but it was time to make some major changes in my life, yet again. I found I wasn't alone with this thinking.

I'd met a few couples who had sold their city business and were now working seasonally in remote areas on cattle stations. One woman was telling me the story of the stress her husband was under running an IT business with twenty staff. She talked him into a new lifestyle. He was very hesitant, IT was all he knew. They began volunteer work on various farms whilst travelling, learning and gaining confidence. This couple now works seasonally on an outback cattle station for the past six years. She cooks meals for the workers and he goes out fixing dam pumps, fences, mustering and branding cattle and all sorts of odd jobs. She told me to look at his face when he returned that afternoon. He arrived back covered in dirt and sweat and his face wore a wide relaxed grin. Joy and enthusiasm for life oozed from every fibre of his body.

I also had the opportunity to chat to several people who were cycling around large parts of Australia. They weren't athletes, it was just a personal journey. At a pace of around 100 kilometres a day, one man had covered over 4,000 kilometres through Central Australia. I'd bumped into him three times and spent a several days talking about the logistics of cycling, what he had experienced and how his journey had changed him.

The last time we met, he was two days from Darwin and had changed his flight back home to Europe three times, delaying the inevitable. He spoke about the changes he was planning to simplify his life for his future. He knew he could not return to the same busy, complex lifestyle he had left six months ago. He also knew most of his friends would not understand why or how his journey changed him. Over a year later we made contact and yes he did make those plans happen by building a solar generated tiny house and more cycling trips in other countries. Letting go of an unfulfilled lifestyle for his own happiness, inner peace and an excitement for experiencing life.

Hopefully, I will stick to that one month rule if something adds or takes away from living a more fulfilled, simpler life. I certainly want a few more creature comforts and space than I currently have. Yet I have to be mindful of not falling back into the 'must have' or the mere wants of the latest version of something trap.

***My aim is to make technology work for me,<br>rather than being technology's slave.***

# Living with the best of the past, present and future

Generations will come and go. Each era will contribute its strengths as the building blocks to our ever evolving heritage. People will face and rise to their own unique set of challenges when they step into the unknown. Holding on to their own strong beliefs that will affect their future.

We can't afford to be ignorantly stuck in the mindset of just one generation. Not our own, the past or the future's. We need to openly accept and learn from each generation's blunders, then try to understand the following generation's views and beliefs and support them wholeheartedly.

I think it's easy to understand our past generations because we can read their completed story. It's also easy to understand our present status because we are in the midst of writing the final chapter of our own story. What is difficult, is trying to see and having faith where the future leads, propelled by our children's beliefs and their first tentative steps on their own journey.

Currently, we are only reading the first chapter, the idea of their journey. Slowly revealing its characters, unfolding plots and the many twists and turns. We can only surmise if 'the butler did it' scenario at this point. The children are clearly ahead of us, busily writing and re writing the drafts of their forward vision that we have yet to see or understand.

This will be their story, their future, the one they have to live in, not ours, so they must make the decisions. We won't know in what areas they will be right or wrong, yet we have to take a step back, support them and respect that this is their journey, not ours. We can only help guide them by being honest, open with our mistakes or downfalls. Passing down our knowledge.

We must also remember that we have all been in their shoes, challenging new ideas and creating new paths contrary to our own parents. So let them explore their ideals. We have already had our turn adding to our heritage. We have to hand over the reins and trust they will be better than us.

Fortunately, my daughter is a Millennial who reminds me often about my own stale beliefs. When we have conversations about current world issues, I see her eyes slightly roll or become distracted when I offer limited and ignorant views on a host of subjects. Indignantly, I raise my eyebrows and think to myself 'I know better!' The harsh reality is I don't.

At times, it hurts me. The real reason it hurts is because it is creating a divide between our relationships and exposes my ignorance, it is not about our views. So the biggest trial for me is to see her world and future through her eyes rather than my own limitations. It's always difficult to alter our ingrained beliefs the older we become, however we need to be flexible in our thinking as we once were at their age.

Whenever I pluck the courage to jump into her world, I find that is the time when she can see and accept any sort of guidance or pieces of criticism of the new generations. We have to make the first moves or we shall be fobbed off, unheard.

***I have to change...she already is the change.***

***Respect the subjects that drives them forward.***

***When we do, we will be able to impart the lessons we have learnt***
***– our advice will be more forthcoming.***

# THE FUTURE LIES IN THESE HANDS

*Our generation will be remembered for the decisions we make today*

## Possibilities of the new era

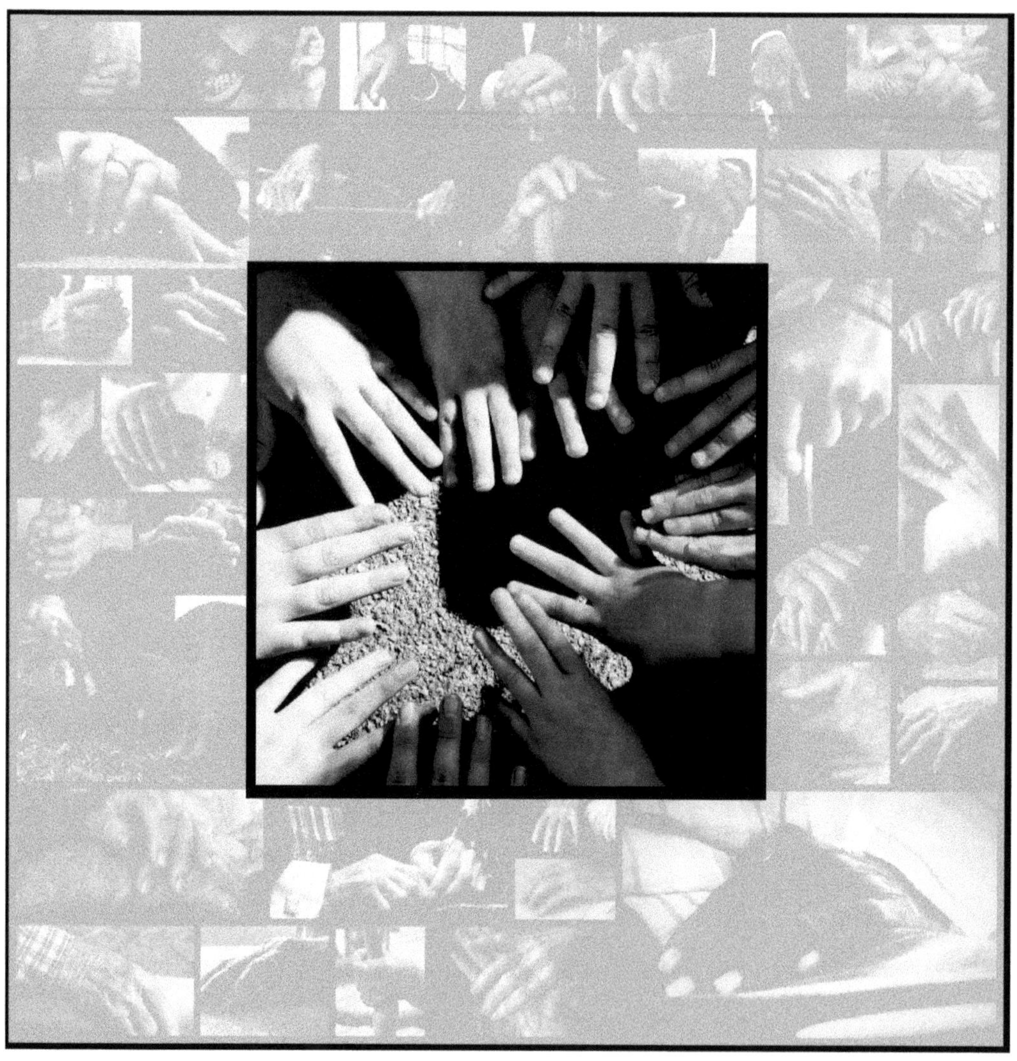

# Be excited for the future

Admitting that we now have a problem is the first step to solving it. Let's take a step back and see how our early Australian spirit of ingenuity and steely determination solved untold problems in our country. By dismissing old standards, creating new thoughts and actions, they were able to boldly move forward in harsh conditions against great odds. We are now faced with another opportunity to draw heavily on our unique traits and become excited for the future. A time for all of us to 'Give it an enormous Go!'

A new era is upon us. Our children are speaking up and taking action demanding to be heard on behalf of their future. This alone is breaking ground as children from prior generations were bought up to only speak when spoken to. There have been many who challenged authorities, yet these young children are having a real impact in the world like no other generation.

***"We must hold the older generations accountable for the mess they have created..."***

They are highly passionate, well informed, and articulate beyond their years. They are well armed with an arsenal of facts from great minds around the world to support their beliefs. They are urgently trying to shift an older generation's mindset in the political and corporate arenas. Children are teaching adults and brutally reprimanding them for their negligence and greed. Demanding they make it a priority to change their ways and policies before it is too late.

One of the major areas our children are taking on is something that is not just bigger than themselves, or more than individual countries or continents. It's a subject larger than any throughout human history – our planet. Just typing this statement feels like an insurmountable burden. Try to imagine how much weight these children feel and carry for their own future!

The subject is very real in their minds and eyes. They possess a compelling argument. They can't wait until they grow up to be the powers to make the changes. They see the clock ticking fast and they alone will pay the ultimate price when the older authorities have passed on.

***"You say you love your children above all else, and yet You are stealing their future in front of their eyes."***

This burning issue is about the destruction of our lands, oceans and atmospheres. It's about our unstainable footprint - our climate crisis. It's believed there will be no recovery for humanity once we pass the tipping point of no return. It's estimated we only have ten years to make drastic changes. It's already time to put on the brakes with the ways we are currently living.

That is a very scary thought, but this is a new era of possibilities if we all make that our focus for the future. There are certainly ones who deny this will occur presenting their own arguments. But do we know for certain who is right at this point?

***Can we really afford to say Ooops down the track?***

***This kind of error may not be reversible.***

***Are we prepared to take that massive gamble through our own selfish needs and ignorance?***

It's an enormous weight on such young shoulders at an age when they should be playing and having fun. But who else will stand up, speak up for their rightful concerns on their future? We have been living a very comfortable, convenient life for the past sixty odd years – at a great cost. It's fairly obvious that our generation's mistake was greed at the sake of the planet. Our resources are not infinite, yet we currently act like they are. It's not a subject that can be lightly dismissed through our own ignorance or ignoring facts.

Is it so unreasonable for them to want what we had? The natural basics we took for granted; clean water, clean air, natural foods, uncontaminated, unpolluted lands and oceans. With the extinction of an alarming number of animal, sea, insect and plant life we will leave them little. How will they answer their own children as to why we didn't do something? Yes, it is a heavy burden for their future created by our own hands. We have become unreasonably selfish with the use of our technological advances, yet we can divert technology for the betterment of our life and planet.

***A shining beacon takes to the world stage.***
***"We are going to change the fate of humanity"***

One passionately concerned young fifteen year old harshly dressed down world leaders in 2018 at the United Nations Climate Change COP24 Conference in Poland. This young climate activist gave a bold, earnest speech. Shaming world powers with brutal honesty on their inactions, greed and politics. Upping the sense of urgency by announcing that this is a Climate Crisis, not a change.

***"You are not mature enough to tell it like it is.***
***Even that burden you leave to us children..."***

This courageous young girl named Greta began skipping school each Friday to sit alone outside her parliament building to create awareness for the plight of the climate crisis. It sparked a worldwide youth school strike for the climate movement in 2018 called Fridays For Future. Within less than a year, over 1.6 million children around the world from over 125 countries joined in the movement and is growing in momentum. "Unite behind the science – that is our demand."

Greta has Asperger's with a laser focus on science facts where she has researched climate change for over six years and is well aware of the hard cold facts. Her parents have wholeheartedly supported their daughter's vision by making dramatic changes in their lives in line with her beliefs for the planet. Living simply, transforming their home to solar energy, growing their own vegetables and cycling as their main mode of transport.

I became aware of Greta's highly passionate mission at the end of my journey. Watching her powerful speech moved me with her sheer bold objective. She has since spoken at the World Economic Forum 2019 and met with a variety of world leaders to discuss solutions. They are listening and some countries have now officially declared our climate as a crisis. Greta and her message for the future is no longer being ignored. We also can't afford to ignore it.

After spending time exploring our own country, I believe our land, our home is worth fighting for, it's the only one we have. There are many who do not believe in our climate crisis or choose to deny the issue as it appears too complex or have ulterior motives. All I can say; are you prepared to take that massive gamble and stand accountable to your children and descendants?

***Our generation will be remembered for the decisions we make today.***

***We can be excited for the future if we make daily changes.***

***Our home is worth fighting for, it's the only one we have.***

# Life can change in a heartbeat

By the time I'd heard about Greta's quest on climate awareness, I was in the final stages of writing this book. I felt it was fitting to introduce the following generation's long journey ahead into the unknown. It would also be the last piece of my own journey's puzzle.

Greta's story solidified the vision I was already working towards for my own future. I needed a home and location to reflect living a less complicated lifestyle with less things surrounding me.

***Living minimally for my trip was out of necessity, then it became a choice.***

***Unaware, I was gradually living a life more aligned and within the means of the planet.***

We have become wasteful consumers with little regard to the planet. My trip forced me to live a less wasteful life. Along this journey, I had to be mindful of everything I used. Learning the simplest forms of power and understanding those wretched amps and watts. Limiting my daily water usage, I can now shower and wash my hair in under three minutes. With limited space, I couldn't afford to buy excessive varieties of food, nor could I afford to waste anything. Recycling was born out of necessity and became a bit of a game. With my two month purchase rule in place, I also resorted to buying items I needed at Opportunity Shops in small country towns and dropping off items I no longer had a use for. It wasn't just a fun way to shop, it felt good and natural not to be wasteful. My own footprint on the planet had shrunk considerably and I hadn't realised it.

***I wanted to live with the best and not the worst of the last, current and future generations.***

***I'm continually finding my Goldilocks mid ground in many areas of life.***

I was taking my new knowledge and experiences for a future home. I've already considered living in a tiny house, renovating a large bus to life on a houseboat, using solar and wind energy. It made so much sense to use the sun rather than creating those excessive power bills everyone is now complaining about. Knowing my daily power consumption, I can easily work out how many batteries and solar panels I would need. I can tolerate the heat and cold far better, eliminating the need for air conditioning. I want a few more comforts and space than my current tiny campervan, but it is unthinkable to return to the excessive commercialism of city living.

I'm also not so precious or as materialistic as I used to be. No longer needing the latest 'whatever' to try to fill an endless commercial void or to impress others with my purchases. I'm filled by a curiosity of continual learning, people's stories, being in absolute awe of our country's landscapes and my own impact to my child's and our country's legacy.

I don't believe we all need to go full 'Hippie' style living, yet we do need to stop being wasteful in all areas of our lives. Understand the consequences of our everyday actions, to respect this planet and think of something much, much bigger than ourselves, the future of humanity.

I still laugh and shake my head thinking back to where I was a few years ago, to where I am now. Physically, mentally and I guess you could call it spiritually. That single idea took me on an incredibly fascinating journey of discovery in many areas I didn't anticipate. It certainly has been an exciting and bumpy ride! I had changed, for the better. I'd better buckle up for the next journey.

***I no longer need the latest 'whatever' to fill an insatiable void.***

***Connecting to the land and seeing something bigger than myself keeps me fulfilled.***

# How will we write our own legacy?

It will be interesting to see what kind of legacy we shall leave to future generations, and how we will be viewed in decades to come. As with all generations, what will they see as our greatest contributions and our biggest mistakes? Only time will tell.

So, how will we write our final chapter? The question is, will it have a happy or a sad ending? Will we be proud of our contributions to our heritage? Or even our own personal legacy to our families. What values will we pass down to our children so they can become better than us?

Australia's foundation was built by countless hands of ordinary individuals who collectively, just happened to do extraordinary things. Their focus was to seize the opportunity to make a better life for themselves and their children and in turn they created something far bigger than themselves, a prosperous nation. There are similarities where we stand today.

***We are those ordinary people who are capable to alter the future for a better life for ourselves and our own children.***

When our children see us taking action, their future will look less uncertain, they will be less anxious. Our own action will propel them into the future with more confidence, with greater decision making.

***Be excited for our future, and leave a legacy you can be proud of***

At this present time, we have to ask ourselves if our home, our planet and future is worth fighting for. Are we prepared to make daily personal changes and demand our powers to make massive changes? We have the technology and ingenuity to alter the current course and we certainly have a strong reference we can make dramatic changes against the odds by our own history's stories.

We can all Give it a Go!

One day, we will be those great grandparents and younger people will want to know about our lives with equal interest. Sit down and write your own stories. Stories that you would be proud to be retell one day. They will be part of your own and our country's history.

***There will always be stories to be told and recorded.<br>Stories reveal who we are today and directs us into the future.***

***Our generation will be remembered for the decisions we make today.<br>...the cycle of change continues.***

**If one man can make a difference so can we**

# One man's selfless gift to humanity

Each of the stories in this book are irreplaceable records and insights into our unique heritage. People create our history, the land is our legacy. There is one more story I'd like to share that has a profound impact for generations to come.

Although I never had the privilege to meet this shy, modest gentleman, I heard his story while visiting Kakadu National Park in the Northern Territory. Firstly, I feel it's important to understand the significance of this area to the story.

Kakadu is one of only 25 UNESCO World Heritage Listed areas in the world noted for both its cultural and natural significance to humanity, it's classed as having "Outstanding Universal Value" to our world. Australia is uniquely home to four of these 25 areas.

It's one of those places that effortlessly transports you back in time with its multitude of dramatic, primal vistas. Looking out over the Nadab Plains in Ubirr at sunset is jaw dropping, a one kilometre hike up a mountain takes you to Gumlon's natural infinity rock pools. There are theatrical scenes of cascading water over ancient escarpments at Twin Falls and Jim Jim Falls. Yellow Water is breath takingly raw with brightly coloured waterways and wetlands filled with an abundance of birdlife and of course crocodiles. The historic cultural records of cave and rock art in Ubirr and Nourlangie are mesmerising natural art galleries. These are just a few places to experience in the extraordinary UNESCO World Heritage Listed Kakadu National Park.

The geological history alone spans more than two billion years. This unique archaeological site documents one of the longest histories of any group in the world with Indigenous creation stories recorded in their cave and rock art. The area has been continuously inhabited by our Indigenous people for more than 50,000 years, making them the world's oldest living culture. Preserving this historical and breathtaking area is vital to Australia's heritage and the world.

To say Kakadu is special to the world would be a vast understatement. Every moment of my stay, I was staggered by the raw, complex ecosystem wilderness of this timeless land. Visitors have access to around five percent of its vast 2 million hectares.It took me over two weeks to not just explore, but to experience parts of this living cultural landscape.

Standing on the outcrop of Stone Country you look across the savanna to Nourlangie where a great number of ancient rock art is preserved. Just beyond Nourlangie sits another cultural site of the Indigenous Djok clan called Koongarra.

One man's passionate journey took over two decades battling a world mining giant who had a lease on this land to mine the rich resources of uranium worth billions of dollars. This one man stood to become one of the wealthiest men in Australia. But his idea of wealth was different to the money he was continually offered to lease the mining rights on his land. He believed in his enormous cultural responsibility as custodian to the land of his ancestors.

***"My responsibility is on the land and I don't own the land.<br>The land owns me."***

Wanting to preserve this land and his beliefs, he tirelessly worked with our federal government to 'gift' the land to Australia. Later, he flew to Paris to plea with UNESCO to have Koongarra included into Kakadu National Park's World Heritage Listing. In 2011 the mining lease was repealed and the land will be forever protected and safe under UNESCO's World Heritage Listing.

The simplicity of his vision:

***"...money comes and goes, but the land is always here"***

***"It will be there for future generations for people all over the world."***

Hearing this story, I wondered how many people would give up such great material wealth for humanity. The temptation to take the money would be an immense burden, yet this man never wavered in his strong cultural beliefs. Each day, he works as a ranger in Kakadu passionately looking after the land he knows, the land he loves and the land he protects.

Sometimes we feel we are too small to sway the tide of society, yet this one man's journey proved we are never too small. His gift to humanity was selfless, sending a message that one person can make a profound difference if you have a strong vision.

This man's name is Jeffery Lee, who is the Traditional Owner of the Djok Clan.

Remember his name for the gift and legacy he gave to us all.

***Ultimately, all life is about the land***

***Humans are a part of nature***

***if we destroy nature we eventually destroy ourselves<br>Our past, present and future always lay in our own hands***

In 1969, the whole world stopped to watch in awe when 'man' took his first step on the moon.

On the second moon landing, around half the world watched, the other half just read about it.

Yet throughout all of time, 'man' never tires watching the all compelling beauty of a sunrise or sunset nature provides on a daily basis.

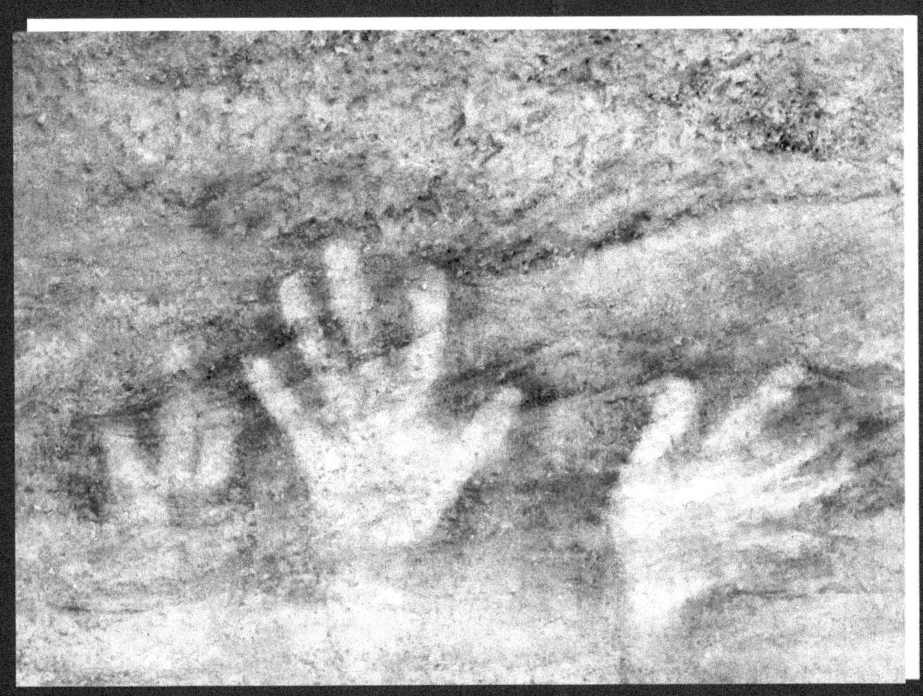

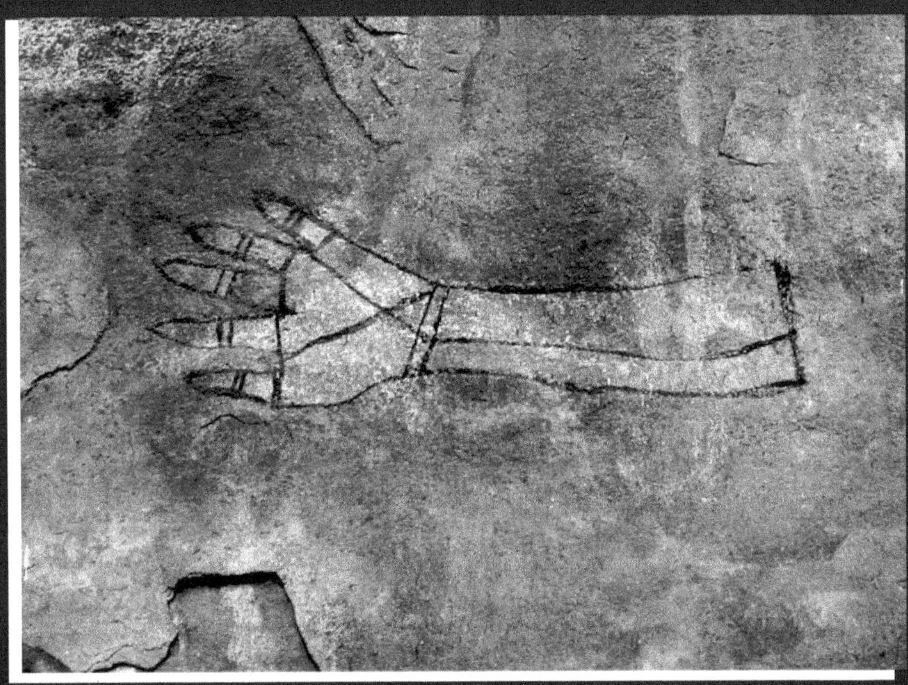

*two cultures meet...*

# Notes:

## Quotes:

*Quotes from the pages ***'The Defenders'***

Wording from chance conversations by a variety of people I met in various towns throughout Australia.

***One man's selfless gift to humanity pages - by Jeffrey Lee.***

Wording from various video clips about his journey to protect Koongarra.

***Be excited for the future pages - by Greta Thunberg.***

Wording from various news video clips and Wikipedia on her speeches.

## Stories:

*With each main story, the people gave permission and fully understood that their stories and images of their hands were for public publication and public use.

**Nursing Home Stories:**

**The majority of the people who lived in the nursing home suffered from varying degrees of dementia. Naturally, conversations were quite limited, yet you learn fascinating snippets of their life over time. Obviously, I wasn't able to gain permission to share people's full stories, images and names for this book as they were not of sound mind to agree. However I'm able to include undisclosed situations I witnessed.

**Permission:**

** It was paramount for the people I met to feel safe and comfortable with me and fully understand the purpose of this book.

**There was also a need to be mindful that elderly people can be vulnerable with strangers, like myself, was important.

I ensured to first contact members of the community so they could search my background. To contact either family members and or neighbours, so they understood my presence and purpose. It was also important that someone they knew and trusted could be present when we met. Although it didn't always happen.

**Book Cover Design** by Lexa Harpell

**Photographic images** by Lexa Harpell and Roberta

# About the Author

Lexa's birthplace is Bondi, Australia – her home is wherever she is in the world. A dear friend once told her, 'Travel and leave a legacy in life' – and so she does. Her books, photography and projects are intertwined, they inspire each other and take her to fascinating places.

With a curious mind and loving diversity in her life, she is mostly travelling 'on the road' capturing images of places and subjects from her surrounds, as well as finding inspiring new projects to work on.

Most recently, her three year project to locate, hear and record stories from people who were the last generation who carved the foundation of modern Australia with their bare hands. To understand what it took to build a nation and learn about the people, our identity and heritage.

Lexa also captures her county's incredible raw beauty with her trusty, well used camera, often hiking in remote places. Her images have been featured and displayed in themed exhibitions.

Another project took her to 34 towns in four countries in Europe. A journey to walk in the steps of her ancestors after an intense research and recordings with her brother. Producing a 500 page living history book for her family and their descendants.

# Other published books

To Mum, Gifts from Your Soul
To Dad, Gifts from Your Soul
Available from Amazon.com

## Links to view her photography

https://lexa-harpell.pixels.com
https://redbubble/lexaharpell.com

www.ingramcontent.com/pod-product-compliance
Ingram Content Group UK Ltd.
Pitfield, Milton Keynes, MK11 3LW, UK
UKHW051129260726
13967UKWH00010B/2953